Every pharma industry profession
simply and clearly explains import:

A very interesting book – a must-have for all professionals operating in life science and marketing with a clear and structured approach to solve real business problems. It is based on Collaborative Creativity: a flexible framework to increase ability to generate and execute meaningful ideas, through the empowerment of people – because the ability to understand and engage others is an awesome superpower.

Nicoletta Luppi, *Senior Vice President and Managing Director MSD Italia*

The Forces of Collaborative Creativity is succinct without being spare. It is in-depth without being murky. It is practical without being uninspired. Truly a book to buy two of: one to keep fresh on the shelf to invite the conversation of others, and one to dogear the crap out of and rip out pages to tape to the walls.

Bruce Rooke, *Director Pufferfish, first-ever recipient of the CLIO Healthcare Lifetime Achievement Award*

Collaborative Creativity provided us with insights that were unimaginable with traditional market research, to the point where, thanks to the depth of understanding of the experience of PKU patients, the company criteria and language of segmentation changed. Subsequently, we were able to share the results with specialist HCPs who welcomed the information on the opinions and needs of their patients and I am sure that they too regard their patients differently now.

Maria Teresa Lerco, *General Manager, Orchard Therapeutics Italia.*

I was privileged to work with Peter Comber as a colleague when he was the Creative Director for Europe at GSW Worldwide. Many of the concepts Peter describes in his book were incubated in that period and made more robust through practised implementation. Now they are proven processes that I have also adopted to manage my medical device business.

Philippe Deschamps, *President and CEO Helius Medical Technologies and former CEO, GSW Worldwide*

The Forces of Collaborative Creativity certainly provides us with an innovative and multidimensional approach to many aspects of our professional needs. This new comprehensive approach perfectly meets the current needs of healthcare professionals, who are increasingly asked to take care of patients in a multidisciplinary manner and as part of a multiprofessional team To achieve this goal, the five forces reported in the book are of utmost importance. Moreover, as times and needs are changing, we have to learn to adopt new tools for monitoring and checking patients remotely; to do this creatively is mandatory. I found this book a very useful guide to change our way of thinking and working.

Professor Marcello Giovannini, MD,
Professor Emeritus of Pediatrics, University of Milan

The brilliance of The Forces of Collaborative Creativity is that it understands the essential catalysts of creativity and the true nature of organizations. Without collaboration, even the most creatively minded organizations wither on the vine. The Forces of Collaborative Creativity energizes and focuses organizations to surprise themselves and the world around them with elegant, powerful and engaging ideas.

Guy Mastrion, President and Chief Creative Officer of
Brandforming and the F. William Harder Chair Professor
of Business Administration at Skidmore College

Collaborative Creativity goes beyond design thinking and market research, on a journey that will bring the reader to discover themselves as creative directors – able to manage their internal and external workshops with professional exercises tailor-made to fit specific requirements.

Marco Mohoric', Digital Medicines Customer
Engagement Manager, Angelini Pharma

This book offers a lot more than its title suggests. Peter's unique methodology, developed over 30 years in healthcare communications, offers insights for every sector of business and society: how to design a framework for collaborative creativity to deliver effective outcomes through social and professional cohesion. Marketing, communications, project management and product innovation professionals have much to learn from his idiosyncratic but easy-to-follow approach.

Julian Boulding, President, the networkone

A practical guide that challenges the orderly way pharma marketing is used to doing things - either when it embarks on launching a new product or when it reinvents a promotional campaign, repeating and improving what has been already done seems almost inevitable. The Forces of Collaborative Creativity vividly shows how we can all leverage our most valuable human assets to seek change in a self-propelling and sustainable fashion.

Rodrigo Fernandez-Baca, General Manager, Seattle Genetics, Italy

'Creativity' is an over-used word, but in The Forces of Collaborative Creativity, Peter Comber shows you the power it can have in fresh ways. His thoughtful, practical and exciting approach supercharges traditional creative processes by enabling and building on creative contributions from all the 'owners' of the problem to be solved – be they citizens, patients, marketers, agency teams, doctors or scientists. Reading this book made me really want to be part of one of the workshops run by Peter and his team!

Matthew Willcox, Founding Partner of The Business of Choice and prizewinning business book author

The Forces of Collaborative Creativity

A practical guide to creative teamwork
in the healthcare business

Peter John Comber

Practical Inspiration
PUBLISHING

First published in Great Britain by Practical Inspiration Publishing, 2020

© Peter John Comber, 2020

The moral rights of the author have been asserted.

ISBN   978-1-78860-151-1   (print)
        978-1-78860-150-4   (epub)
        978-1-78860-149-8   (mobi)

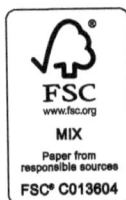

Practical Inspiration
PUBLISHING

FSC
www.fsc.org
MIX
Paper from
responsible sources
FSC® C013604

To Alessandra and George

Contents

About the author

Peter John Comber is an expert on creativity.

He began working in graphic design and advertising in 1983 and for more than 30 years he has created all manner of things for all manner of brands.

Early on, he became interested in computers and was online before the birth of the web. In 1994 he designed his first website which led to him founding his first company, a digital agency. His next venture was a healthcare advertising agency that he co-founded together with a leading US healthcare advertising network. Within this collaboration, he later took on the role of European Creative Director. In 2013, he created Atstrat, a healthcare consultancy dedicated to Collaborative Creativity and in 2016 it was expanded to include patient support and advocacy services.

Peter's career has always been in applied creativity. This has allowed him to develop the theory and practice of Collaborative Creativity with his:

- vast personal experience of creative work with groups of various sizes

- observations of what makes it easier or harder to have ideas

- expertise in directing the creative activities of large, international, heterogeneous groups of people

- understanding of the complexities and pratfalls of taking an idea from concept to realization within large, complex and multicultural corporations.

Peter believes that creativity is a force for change and a fundamental human characteristic. He also believes that applied creativity must embrace diversity and allow ideas to evolve to be relevant to different people and ultimately successful, and that collective creativity is an effective, efficient and enjoyable way of solving complex problems and creating the right environment for the solution to be embraced.

More information about Peter's career can be found at https://peter-comber.net/pjc-career.html.

Acknowledgements

Writing this book has been one of the most demanding things I have ever done and I am convinced I would have given up without the infinite support and encouragement of my wife and my business partner.

I am lucky to have worked with many people in many countries and everyone with whom I've created something has taught me something. There is a part of them all in the ideas expressed in this book.

I am still amazed by the generosity of the people who agreed to read the first draft of this book and provide constructive criticism. Without their precious comments, I would be embarrassed by rather than proud of the final result.

As the author, I am but a small cog in the large mechanism required to get this book into your hands. I am grateful for the professional skill and good old-fashioned pleasantness of the extended team at Practical Inspiration Publishing.

A huge thank you to all the clients who have trusted in me and the power of creativity. Long may they continue to profit from the forces of Collaborative Creativity.

A brief introduction to Collaborative Creativity

For more than 35 years, my job has required me to be creative every day and also to help others to be creative. In that time, I have learnt more than most people about ideas and the creative process. When I began my career, there was a clear distinction in most working environments between those whose job it was to be creative and everyone else. That has changed, with approaches such as design thinking and co-creation contributing to a shift in the ways businesses employ creativity. Today, far more people in diverse roles are expected to be creative because creativity produces ideas, ideas start innovation and innovation generates revenue and profits. Yet creativity is much more than a raw material that can be refined into practical inventions: it is a powerful force that can change the beliefs we hold, modify the physical reality we inhabit and influence culture and interpersonal relations.

Collaborative Creativity is applied creativity. It is a method that involves groups of people working together to solve business problems. I developed the concept of Collaborative Creativity while working as a consultant with pharmaceutical companies in numerous countries in Europe and North America and the methodology has since been refined through many diverse projects that have involved people from all over the world.

Collaborative Creativity is a flexible framework that has many applications. As the name suggests, it has two constants: collaboration and creativity. Consequently, in this book you will learn about ways to help groups of people work together to generate new ideas. Unlike other creative approaches, Collaborative Creativity will also help you appreciate and make use of the by-products of creative activity.

I use the term 'by-products' provocatively here, because creativity produces more than just ideas and the secondary products it generates can be equally useful and valuable. I argue that if you want to use creativity to its full effect in your business, you need to know how to take advantage of all the products of creativity – or, as I prefer to call them, the *forces of creativity*. I consider them forces because, when they are operating to their full effect, they directly result in various kinds of change. I have observed Collaborative Creativity consistently produce five forces, which we will examine in detail in this book. They are shown in Figure 1.

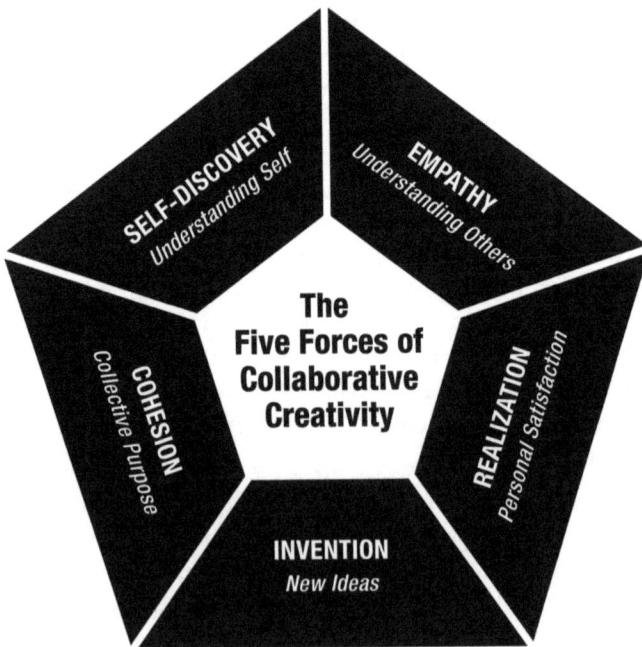

Figure 1: The five forces of Collaborative Creativity

Collaborative Creativity always produces ideas. Sometimes the ideas are the primary goal; at other times they are a means to an end – for example, a way to help people understand something about themselves or others. Often, the aim is to produce practical ideas while also achieving another objective, such as the cohesion and motivation of a group of people. In business today, I think there is a certain dogma around the use of creativity: it has to produce 'useful' ideas that can be monetized as quickly as possible. As a business owner, I understand the legitimate need to achieve a return on investment, but a focus on ideas as the only product of creativity ignores other valuable outcomes. Creativity produces ideas *and so much more*.

We humans are not rational beings. We are all guilty of deception – more often than not it is self-deception. If you are uncomfortable with that statement and are not familiar with the research and writing of Dan Ariely, I strongly recommend you read his work – I suggest you start with his book *Predictably Irrational* (see details in the Further Resources section at the end of the book).

Most adults are accomplished talkers and can discuss a topic in a convincing and apparently logical way. This skill gets elevated to an art form by those who practise competitive debating or by lawyers or advocates, for whom it is part of their professional competence.

It is fascinating – and useful to know – that while language seems to be controlled at a very conscious and rational level in our brains, creative thinking occurs in deeper and more ancient areas of the brain. The ideas you have reveal something about you. Creative thought accesses deeper areas of our minds than those concerned with logic and language, so its manifestations can show you unexpected, unconscious beliefs, emotions and internal contradictions. Once those ideas are out in the open, they can be discussed and understood. Creativity tends to be a (relatively) honest process.

The act of thinking creatively about a problem for a certain period of time changes your relationship with that problem. The change may be only slight or it may be quite significant, but whenever you are challenged in the right way to focus on a given subject or problem, it makes you elaborate new theories and explore new possibilities. When this happens, your own ideas can surprise you and the ideas and experiences of others can inspire you and lead you in unexpected directions that can further modify your own beliefs and even shed light on beliefs and values that are on a preconscious level. Creativity changes the creator.

We tend to value and even over-value the things we create. Having an original thought or finding a solution to a problem is inherently rewarding. When we create something, we feel satisfaction. Ideas that form within a group have an advantage over ideas produced by an individual: there are more people who want 'their' idea to succeed. In this way, Collaborative Creativity cultivates a sense of co-authorship. This is significant because co-authorship means both sharing the ownership of an idea and also the satisfaction that comes from having contributed towards its creation. Furthermore, shared ownership of an idea can give a group a common purpose in its development, dramatically increasing the motivation of the group's members and improving results. Creativity both rewards and motivates.

Creativity also affects human relationships. Something profound happens to people who share and develop ideas together: the creative process involves a transfer of energy and a kind of intellectual intimacy. Following the thoughts of another and contributing your own thoughts towards a shared goal is a powerful way of uniting people. In the right setting, human relationships can be strengthened and the sharing of personal beliefs and values can be accelerated. In the twenty-first century – a time already defined by its rapid change – the intelligence of an organization is not defined by the IQ or the experience of its individuals, but rather by the speed and effectiveness with which they are able to collaborate, test and adopt new ideas in the context of a shared purpose. Creativity unites.

For the most part, pharmaceutical companies are driven by science and organized with rigid processes in place. It's fair to say that pharmaceutical companies aren't particularly creative environments. So you may be wondering, 'Who is going to do all this creativity?'

The answer is anybody and everybody, because everyone is creative. Often creativity is erroneously associated with being artistic, but creativity is not craft: it is a basic human ability and we all do it. Dreams are ample proof, if any were needed, that combining things in unusual ways and creating stories (imagining alternative versions of the past, present or future) are something that the human brain is built to do. Our brain is creative – it literally does this while we sleep.

Anyone can be creative, given the right questions and stimuli, together with a safe environment and the right motivation to share their ideas. I have seen people who don't consider themselves creative and who identify as introverts being very productive and producing innovative work within a group. They were able to do this so well because the problem they were asked to consider was tailored to their own experience.

If you are a caregiver, you will have relevant practical and emotional experience about managing a certain disease or condition. If you are given a creative challenge that is pertinent to that experience, your creative approach and ideas will easily be inspired by that experience. If you are a medical liaison of a pharmaceutical company, you will have your own experience of the profession, your specific role and the pathology in which you specialize. Again, if you are given a creative challenge that is pertinent to that experience, your creative approach and ideas will be inspired by that experience.

If you put the caregiver and the medical liaison to work together on a creative challenge that is pertinent to their combined experience, their creative approach and ideas will be inspired by the confluence of their minds.

The creative approach and ideas of each individual are the product of their unique experience, so when you combine different creative approaches you get different ideas. This is why group creativity can be so powerful and produce valuable results that combine different perspectives. With the right questions as a spark, and the right setting as kindling, each individual's personal experience is the fuel that feeds the creative fire of the group.

For valid reasons, healthcare is obsessed with demonstrable facts. Human behaviour, on the other hand, is influenced more by emotion than by facts. In his book, *Descartes' Error: Emotion, Reason, and the Human Brain*, neuroscientist Antonio Damasio brilliantly challenges traditional ideas about the connection between emotions and rationality. Damasio has studied people with brain damage that impairs their emotional functioning and found that they are unable to make decisions. Given two choices of similar foods, they can't decide which to eat, despite being able to describe in logical terms the decision they have been asked to make. Emotions play a highly significant role in our choices and therefore our actions. When scientific evidence proves that facts and logic are trumped by emotion, even the most science-driven culture must accept that, as a means of understanding and using emotion, creativity is indispensable when it comes to achieving healthcare goals such as therapeutic adherence or the adoption of healthy lifestyle choices.

In summary, I believe Collaborative Creativity has transformational power that derives from the sum of its five forces (Figure 1), and each of these forces produces effects that have valuable applications in business in general and pharmaceutical companies in particular. I believe this because I have witnessed it, and in the next chapter I will share one of my practical experiences with you.

1 The foundations of Collaborative Creativity

The five forces of Collaborative Creativity

I once sent a dozen doctors back in time. It was a creative exercise, a thought experiment designed to help understand the present. The group comprised several highly qualified hospital specialists, who I'd engaged on behalf of a client who wanted to understand their perceptions of the implications on their practice of recent medical advances. The client had an impressive list of achievements and wanted to make sure that these were fully appreciated by the prescribers of their products. At the top of the list was the client's proudest achievement: the first cure for a serious chronic disease. I divided the physicians into four teams and gave each team an identical task: 'Knowing what you know today, write the bullet points of a speech presented at a medical congress five years in the past, in which you – time travelling specialists from the future – tell your colleagues about how their practice will change over the next five years.'

The speeches created by the four teams were very similar, with only minor differences. The majority of the achievements on the client's list were mentioned and the impact of these achievements on the physicians' practice was evident. Yet one item on the list was missing from all four speeches: no team told its colleagues from the past about the cure. The single most important thing from the client's perspective was completely absent from the specialists' description of their colleagues' future. Once the last team had finished presenting its speech notes to the group, I pointed out the missing piece of news and immediately witnessed 12 shocked and puzzled faces.

In the group discussion that followed, the reasons for the omission emerged quickly and were universally recognized by the participants. The key points were, first, that the cure halted the progression of the disease but didn't undo the damage already done to the patient's organs and, second, that the arrival of the cure had seriously disrupted and complicated their clinical practice.

There was a lot of energy in the room: the physicians were excited and intellectually engaged, and they were enjoying thinking about their job in a new way. There was also palpable emotion – the barrier between professional opinion and personal belief had been shattered by the Collaborative Creativity exercise and some inconvenient truths were shared.

The whole exercise, including the discussion at the end, took just over an hour. It was immensely informative and supplied vital insights to the client. Prior to this, the client had a certain attitude towards the market, but after learning about the clinicians' experience and emotions they were able to correctly interpret other signals from the market and their attitude changed.

The client's list of achievements could easily have been turned into a series of questions and the specialists could have been interviewed live, over the phone or even via an online multiple-choice survey. I have no doubt that they would all have given a positive response to a question about the cure. A standard interview could not have achieved the same result. Without the Collaborative Creativity format, the dominant emotional aspects of the evolution of the specialists' clinical practice would have remained hidden beneath impersonal, rational conversation. The physicians also surprised themselves with their work and enjoyed themselves. While traditional market research is usually a boring form of interrogation – not unpleasant, but completely unedifying – Collaborative Creativity sessions (the name of workshops that utilize Collaborative Creativity exercises) are a positive and valuable experience for participants. The day after the Collaborative Creativity session, I invited the participants to take an anonymous online survey, and all responded. Of the specialists, 75% declared that they had learnt something new and 91.6% said they had enjoyed the experience.

This example illustrates what a single Collaborative Creativity exercise can achieve. It was one of five creative exercises in a Collaborative Creativity session that lasted six hours and produced all five forces discussed in this book.

The participants enjoyed the effects of *self-discovery*: they learnt something about themselves. The client felt the force of *empathy*: it was quite a shock to fully understand the perspective of the prescribers of their product. The client also benefited from the force of *invention*: the physicians produced many ideas for things that could improve their work. The participants were rewarded by the force of *realization*: completing the Collaborative Creativity exercises gave them an enjoyable feeling of intellectual achievement. Finally, the physicians felt the force of *cohesion*: when they left the session, they had a stronger understanding of the challenges they shared with their colleagues and consequently a stronger bond.

Not all of the five forces were equally strong, partly because not all were desired – some were by-products. The Collaborative Creativity session was designed to meet the objectives of the client, which were firmly focused on empathy (they wanted to understand their customers) and invention (they wanted to collect new ideas for services to offer their customers). The secondary effects of the session were not a priority, but it is important to note that they were nonetheless positive and in the case of self-discovery indispensable. Without the force of self-discovery the force of empathy would have been greatly diminished.

In a rational conversation, people can only articulate that of which they are consciously aware. In this example, Collaborative Creativity generated the force of self-discovery that amplified the force of empathy.

Even the forces of realization and cohesion – which were not, in this case, necessary for the success of the session – were valuable. The participants were aware that the session had been commissioned by the pharmaceutical company for which I worked. It was an event associated with that brand, so if the experience had been uninspiring or negative, this would have reflected badly on the client. By choosing Collaborative Creativity, my client was able to realize their own goals while also offering a positive experience to their customers.

In summary, Collaborative Creativity always generates the five forces. Their relative strength varies due to the design of a Collaborative Creativity session that privileges one or more forces in pursuit of a given objective.

Self-discovery

The force of self-discovery concerns ideas of self. It emanates from learning and mindfulness, and is useful for revealing the preconscious, irrational drivers of actions, habits, preconceptions, self-image and cognitive bias. (A cognitive bias is an error in interpretation made by the brain, often caused by a simplification of information processing. It is a short-cut that helps us to rapidly make sense of the world and reach decisions.) However, because the decisions are the result of a short-cut, rather than fully reasoned thought, the judgement is sometimes faulty. All these have an enormous effect on perception and actions; in many situations, they are far more influential than logic or reason in decision-making.

If we believe that logic and reason don't exclusively control beliefs and decision-making, and we also believe that civilized verbal communication is strongly controlled by conscious reason, it follows that having a logical conversation with someone about their beliefs and decision-making processes will not tell us anything particularly revealing or useful. Creative exercises that stimulate non-verbal means of expression and indirect exploration are required for self-discovery.

Recently, on behalf of a client, I worked with a non-profit organization that helps people with mental disorders. The objective was to explore the experience of the operators who worked for the organization and the people they assisted to try to identify a new tool to support their efforts.

I organized three Collaborative Creativity sessions. The first lasted six hours and saw the participation of the operators and directors of the NGO. The creative exercises were designed to focus on self-discovery (primarily their frustrations), empathy (their understanding of the people they assisted and the collective and individual emotional burden of mental disorder) and invention (what they wanted to change). The result was a snapshot of the essence of the organization from the perspective of different internal functions. The image it provided was multifaceted but well defined, and it highlighted many crucial aspects of assisting people with mental disorders and the strengths of the organization in this respect.

Using this rich information, I designed a different Collaborative Creativity session that lasted three hours and involved people diagnosed with schizophrenia, bipolar disorder and severe depression. The creative exercises were designed to focus on self-discovery (their relations with others and within the NGO), empathy (their experience of their condition) and invention (what they wanted to change). The output was a surprisingly coherent mirror image of the results of the previous session.

With minor modifications to accommodate the diversity of the participants, I ran a third Collaborative Creativity session that involved people diagnosed with generalized anxiety disorder. The output of this session confirmed and enhanced the results of the other two sessions.

Collecting and analysing the output of the three sessions allowed me to see something interesting. There were many ideas for innovation, and the more viable ideas were new activities or enhancements of existing activities; however, the most interesting result emerged from the area of self-discovery. Almost without exception, the participants mentioned the importance of sharing experiences with their peers. This was important in so many different ways for everyone involved, and it was also part of the heritage of the organization, which had facilitated peer-to-peer interactions for decades. Yet as these were in the form of conversations, there remained no permanent record of them.

Sharing experiences was also a component of the three Collaborative Creativity sessions, and I had witnessed its power at first hand. The two sessions that involved participants with mental disorders included a collage exercise. The group with generalized anxiety disorder performed the exercise in a normal manner, but an overwhelming majority of those in the other group didn't make a collage; instead, they chose exclusively to write.

An idea emerged to create a writing exercise that would solidify the concept of 'testimony of personal experience' that was universally identified as one of the organization's core values, and that was proven to effectively assist the recovery of people with mental disorders.

Working with psychiatrists, we created a formal framework for the exercise and a methodology for collecting and disseminating the positive experiences from adversity of those with mental disorders. This new service has become an integral part of the organization's modus operandi and the 'virtual library' where the stories are collected and read has given tangible permanence to an important aspect of its work. Participation is voluntary, yet in the first three months a total of 86 personal stories were written; the creation of each of them was an exercise in self-discovery. I conducted brief interviews with some of those who wrote their stories, which confirmed that such writing is a rewarding activity that raises self-awareness of the personal progress made in management of and recovery from their condition. It is one of the projects on which I am most proud to have worked.

One area where self-discovery is especially important is understanding patient behaviour and attitudes towards their condition and therapy. The problem of therapeutic non-compliance is massive. Up to 50% of all prescribed drugs are not taken correctly. Consider the contraceptive pill, a drug where the patient is healthy and strongly self-motivated. It is a highly effective drug; fewer than one in 100 women get pregnant in a year when using the pill correctly. The number for 'typical use' (real-world use) is different, though: approximately nine in 100 women using the pill become pregnant each year.[1]

There are many reasons why people don't engage with their condition and their therapies. Some are practical, but many are emotional and behavioural. Even some practical reasons can be identified as rational excuses employed to justify irrational behaviour.

Mathew Willcox, whose book, The Business of Choice: Marketing to Consumers' Instincts, is another that I strongly recommend (see Further Resources section) explains it nicely:

> The areas of human nature this touches upon are known by behavioural
> scientists as hedonic utility (the pleasurable reward that comes from
> an action or choice) and hyperbolic discounting (the innate tendency
> of humans to be swayed more by a smaller reward or consequence in

---

[1] NHS, 'How effective is contraception at preventing pregnancy? Your contraception guide' (2017), www.nhs.uk/conditions/contraception/how-effective-contraception [accessed 2 June 2020].

the present than by a larger one in the future). In general, humans are intuitively drawn more to actions that give them pleasure now, than those that offer functional benefits in the long term — even if they know the longer term gain would have greater value.

If you need to understand why people who use your product act in certain ways, Collaborative Creativity and the power of self-discovery can help you discover how, for example, things like hedonic utility (the total amount of pleasure produced by the act) and hyperbolic discounting (taking a smaller but more immediate reward) are affecting them. Furthermore, once they are aware of it, you can immediately ask them to imagine possible solutions to combat this behaviour.

The cost of innovative treatments and the need for healthcare systems to remain economically sustainable conspire to increase the pressure on pharmaceutical companies to prove the overall value of their products. As compliance is an important component of the efficacy, and consequently the value, of a treatment, it is becoming increasingly common for pharmaceutical companies to offer patient support programmes (PSP) and patient adherence programmes (PAP) in support of their products. Sometimes the formulation of the treatment or the complexity of a medical device can make medication administration a key issue that can be resolved with training or home-based nursing support. However, in those situations where patient attitude is the cause of non-compliance, in order to be able to design an effective PSP it is important to first understand the typical mindsets of specific cohorts of patients and the challenges they face.

By now it shouldn't surprise you that I believe patient or caregiver interviews only scratch the surface when it comes to unearthing information. With Collaborative Creativity, we can use the power of self-discovery to understand the beliefs, behaviours, emotions and needs of patients before designing a PSP or PAP. I am also convinced that the involvement of patients (and other stakeholders) in the design of a programme that aims to help them can make a huge difference to its acceptance and effectiveness. Whenever possible, it is also preferable to work with patient advocacy groups (PAGs), which always appreciate the bottom-up and inclusive approach of Collaborative Creativity.

Learning from those directly involved, to understand which barriers they face in managing their condition and how they believe they could most benefit from assistance, can also accelerate the time it takes to bring a project to market. A Collaborative Creativity session is much quicker and cheaper than a pilot PSP/PAP, but it can achieve similar results. Unlike a pilot, a Collaborative Creativity session is under no pressure to produce a certain result and in extreme cases can simply conclude that the adherence problem can't be resolved in a cost-effective manner. This may be an unfortunate conclusion, but it is usually preferable to arrive at it quickly and with a contained investment compared with a pilot programme.

In these examples of the force of self-discovery, the protagonists are patients and doctors; however, please don't assume that this force is of use only with stakeholders outside pharmaceutical companies. As we shall see later, self-discovery has a role to play in many different kinds of projects that involve all manner of participants, including those who work in pharmaceutical companies.

In summary, self-discovery is a bit like an extraordinary condiment: it's not the food you actually ordered but without it the dish would be bland and forgettable.

Empathy

The force of empathy concerns ideas about others. It is about gathering and transmitting the experience of others. Our actions towards others are influenced by our ideas about them; empathy and compassion bring the ability to achieve better interactions.

In Collaborative Creativity sessions, the force of empathy works in one of two ways. In the first, the creativity from the session allows a third party to comprehend the feelings/thoughts/needs of the participants (an example of this is the time-travelling doctors described previously, where the creative exercises that the physicians completed allowed my client to finally appreciate their true professional experience). The design of the creative exercises focuses on the expression and transmission of personal experience.

In the second, the creativity in the session focuses on understanding and interpreting the feelings/thoughts/needs of a third party – for example, in a Collaborative Creativity session that involved staff from various functions at the client's company, the output of the time-travelling doctors was used as stimuli in creative exercises that focused on inventing a coordinated response to the issues raised by the physicians. The design of the creative exercises focuses on the comprehension and contextualization of the experience of others.

As science discovers therapies for rare and ultra-rare diseases, even the most knowledgeable corporations can find themselves dealing with patient populations with which they are unfamiliar, and which are obscure even for the specialists who see the very few patients with that condition. Collaborative Creativity can provide a psycho-emotional snapshot of the population. Knowledge of the patient experience and mindset can inform a pharmaceutical company's decisions concerning patient support and potentially also turn into information that is of interest and use to healthcare specialists. Sometimes a caregiver is equally or entirely responsible for the management of a patient's condition. The caregiver is usually a loved one who shares the burden of emotions and the practical needs of the disease and its treatment. In this context, the emotions in play are particularly complex and powerful. The work that Collaborative Creativity does with these kinds of participants is designed to provide a constructive and safe channel for their emotions.

One project on which I worked involved caregivers of children with a very rare, severe and degenerative neurologic syndrome for which there is no cure. All the caregivers who participated were parents of these very sick children; sadly, their hopes were limited to diminishing the symptoms and delaying the progression of the disease.

One of the objectives of the Collaborative Creativity session I ran was to create a 'mood board', which is a collection of images, text and sometimes objects that together convey a general idea or feeling about a subject and also indicate how it manifests itself (what it looks like, sounds like, feels like, etc.). Mood boards are an effective tool for describing complex emotional situations to those who have no experience of the situation. Previously, the client had produced some patient materials that hadn't been well received by caregivers. Various caregivers had told the client, 'You don't get it. All these materials do is show you know nothing about the reality of living with this disease.'

Ouch. After the Collaborative Creativity session, the client threw the old materials away. The mood board described a completely different reality from that in the old materials. Values such as joy and hope were depicted by the caregivers in ways that we would never have imagined, but that made perfect sense to the caregivers. Through various exercises (not just the mood board), Collaborative Creativity allowed the caregivers to express their experience in a way that could be appreciated by others. There is an important point here concerning the transfer of empathy. I was careful to condense and organize the emotions of a full-day session into a summary, while maintaining the power and rawness of the emotions for the benefit of those who didn't have direct contact with the participants. In presenting the results of the session, the creative exercises used to record emotion became broadcasters of emotion so the feelings of the participants came alive for the client.

The materials produced by the client following this session (including, in the United States, an online caregiver community) were successful with the caregivers because they finally saw authentic, credible and relevant situations. They also helped to establish the client's reputation with physicians as knowledgeable experts in the field.

In pursuit of customer insights, I have spent thousands of hours in small, dark rooms, peering through one-way mirrors, wearing earphones to listen to conversations constrained by discussion guides. I have observed individual interviews, focus groups and concept testing, and I have presided over advisory boards. The setting, the format and the objective change but they all have one common denominator: dialogue. It is true that innovations such as eye-tracking and other forms of technology are sometimes used and do make a difference; however, in the pharmaceutical sector, the bulk of qualitative research is still done through a formal interview that is almost completely devoid of emotion.

Despite this, my experience of observing various forms of qualitative market research in many different countries has been positive. The results are often fascinating, always informative but also frequently a little frustrating. A brief dialogue between strangers is a weak instrument for discovering deep truths, because people lie. They lie through social convention and through politeness. They lie to themselves – possibly more than they lie to others. They lie to protect or project their own self-image. They lie to cover previous lies. They lie because they don't know, don't care and just want to move on to the next question and the end of the interview. Even innocent four-year-old children lie!

Many years ago, I created the character toys for Kinder Surprise. It was a fun job, imagining whole worlds, the creatures within them and the stories of their adventures. Ferrero, the client, always did extensive research and I would often observe, in order to learn more about what kids liked and disliked, and why. The research covered various age groups, and the youngest group consisted of the four-year-olds – liars every one of them, not through any desire to trick us but because they wanted to please us. Every toy we gave every child was diligently played with (albeit with varying levels of enthusiasm) and when asked if they liked it, every child said, 'Yes!' The only way to discover their true preference was to have two children play together, one with Character A and the other with Character B. After the useless ritual of asking them whether they liked their toy, we would ask them whether they wanted to keep the toy or swap it for the toy the other child had. Interestingly, their answer was usually physical: they would hold the toy close to their body if they wanted to keep it or hold it out in their hand towards the other child if they wanted to swap. Fascinating stuff!

These early experiences led me to the simple notion that, even in market research, actions are more truthful than words. Creative exercises that require some form of action (even if it is just intellectual) can reveal emotions and beliefs that otherwise remain unspoken. Role-playing, for example, is usually effective. If you ask someone why they don't adhere to a prescription, they are likely to offer mostly excuses. If you ask the same person to try to imagine the reasons why a third person might not adhere to the same prescription, they will use their personal experience to provide answers.

I used this kind of technique in a project regarding a rare genetic disease called phenylketonuria (PKU). PKU is a metabolic disorder: in layman's terms, people with PKU are incapable of processing proteins, and if undetected and untreated this results in a build-up of toxic levels of phenylalanine with potentially serious consequences. In approaching this subject, I was fortunate to have the support of four patient advocacy groups. Unlike most of my work, which is covered by confidentiality agreements, you can read the results of this experience in detail because it has recently been published, in collaboration with the Clinical Psychology Department of Health Sciences at the University of Milan.[2]

I won't repeat here the content of the study, which is available through open access, but I would like to point out that the exercise named 'Lifebelt' employed the third-person technique. It asked the participants – all of whom were PKU patients – to invent a metaphoric lifebelt that could provide different types of practical help to other PKU patients struggling to manage the condition. In the study, you will see that other exercises with different approaches were used. They all focused on empathy – even those that may appear to focus on invention. As mentioned previously, sometimes an idea is a means to an end, not the end in itself. Another aspect of this work that is worth noting is that there were two Collaborative Creativity sessions: the first enrolled people who were compliant in managing their condition and the second enrolled people who were not compliant. This format ensured that the tasks were relevant to the participants and is why there were variations in the creative exercises used in the two sessions.

It is especially difficult to obtain insights from medical doctors for reasons that are, perversely, professional. When they are interviewed for market research, they are being consulted, which means they are paid for their opinions and what they say is usually being recorded. Unsurprisingly, the responses they provide tend to be extremely guarded, their words are measured and the content of their replies tends to reflect their professional opinion in a logical and rational way. They are extremely well-trained experts.

Professional opinion is intellectually based and formed by education and official opinions of one's peers. A physician's personal beliefs are influenced by their real-world clinical experience – their place of work, their colleagues, their patients, their schedule, their personal character and ambition all influence the application of theoretical medical knowledge. Personal belief is based on experience and pragmatically driven, so it doesn't always perfectly match professional opinion. To complicate matters further, personal beliefs are not always conscious. We are not always aware of our beliefs; often they manifest themselves as emotions and not as articulated thoughts – as the previous example of time-travelling physicians illustrated.

Collaborative Creativity sessions can bypass the 'consulting mentality' and access real-world experiences and the convictions they produce.

A format that is always very well received is of a session that starts by presenting a summary of the output of a Collaborative Creativity session conducted previously with a cohort of the types of patients the physicians treat regularly. Following this, the information presented is used as stimuli in creative exercises designed to help the participants explore the ramifications of the insights into the patient experience and imagine new approaches. Some aspects of this are similar to a traditional advisory board, but the creative format makes it a more involving experience and the qualitative research used as stimuli – also derived from a Collaborative Creativity session – grounds it in real-world experience. As proof of the effects of this kind of work, I know of one specialist clinic that significantly modified the setting in which they received patients in an attempt to improve their experience and compliance shortly after working on this aspect in a Collaborative Creativity session of this type.

Empathy is a powerful force. It can be extremely influential and its effects can be very positive. It is also ubiquitous in Collaborative Creativity, as you will see in the course of this book. Empathy is generated, transferred or required in many different scenarios. It is essential to successful human interactions, so it is indispensable in any service industry. In summary, empathy is like a map: it is only a representation of something else, yet without it, in unfamiliar territory, you are lost.

Invention

The force of invention is the energy of useful ideas. It is the spark that, under the right conditions, becomes innovation. Invention uses the collective intelligence and imagination of groups to evoke diverse possibilities and analyse them to select the best option. It is also the exchange, dissemination and adoption of ideas that are required for change to occur in organizations. Invention is the force that solves problems.

Collaborative Creativity has been forged by my experience in two industries: advertising and pharmaceuticals. Advertising is a service industry and pharmaceuticals is a manufacturing industry. Like manufacturing in general, the pharmaceutical industry has changed a lot and continues to evolve by offering services that complement products and deepen relationships with customers by providing more value; however, massive opportunities remain.

Somebody once asked me, 'Does creativity sell?' In the context of the discussion, they were challenging the need for creativity since they believed that in pharmaceutical prescription choice the proven facts were all that mattered. The answer I gave was, 'Facts don't change minds, minds change facts.'

When I said this, I was thinking of a cognitive bias called the 'backfire effect' that causes people who encounter evidence contrary to their beliefs to reject facts and strengthen their conviction that their original belief is right. This makes the task of arguing against that person's belief not only difficult but possibly counter productive.

There is plenty of proof of the backfire effect, one study, looking at messages in vaccine promotion,[3] examined the reaction of parents to messages designed to reduce vaccine misperceptions for measles-mumps-rubella (MMR) vaccine. The result concluded that exposure to the facts 'decreased intent to vaccinate among parents who had the least favourable vaccine attitudes'.

Research from Bain & Company[4] tells us that physicians' drug prescription choices are influenced only 50 to 60% by the efficacy, safety and side-effect profile of a drug (and the influence of these factors is trending negatively). The remaining 40 to 50% is based on 'a range of physician and patient experience factors'. Evidently, product characteristics are essential, but other elements are increasingly influential in the overall commercial performance of medicines. Unlike other types of product, upgrades and restyles are rarely a viable option for pharmaceuticals, while the innovation and improvement of services that are part of the physician and patient experience are feasible and relatively easy to execute.

---

[3] B. Nyhan, J. Reifler, S. Richey and G. L. Freed, 'Effective messages in vaccine promotion: A randomized trial', *Pediatrics*, 133 (4) (2014), e835–e842.
[4] Bain, 'How Agile is powering healthcare innovation', www.bain.com/insights/how-agile-is-powering-healthcare-innovation [accessed 2 June 2020].

Let me provide an example of an experience where, initially, literally the only thing that existed was the product. The client was a top 10 pharmaceutical company; the opportunity was the creation of a new business unit dedicated to biosimilars – an entirely new area of activity for the company. The work covered the definition of the initial concept and scope of the business unit prior to the necessary investment approval by the company's board of directors and continued up to the launch of its first product.

As always, confidentiality obligations prevent me from going into details, but at the time biosimilars were new and there were significant aspects of market education for the new offerings to be correctly assessed, used and adopted. Furthermore, the originator biologic therapy had developed a range of services around its product that made switching to a biosimilar (essentially the same therapy) an unequal proposition unless a similar level of services was established. Putting all this together required many diverse competencies and lots of people. Some of these were new to the company, others were veterans of the company for whom the area of biosimilars was new.

Collaborative Creativity allowed different areas of expertise and diverse characters to merge their knowledge, to quickly understand each other, to approach the task as a cohesive group and to construct an operational model that was built around market realities and that reflected the knowledge and views of all stakeholders. From defining the strategy of the business to defining the logo of the first product, the use of Collaborative Creativity allowed the project to advance quickly and with a consensus and mutual understanding that (for the most part!) made the execution fluid and efficient.

In this example, the objective of Collaborative Creativity was to define the characteristics of a start-up and help a group of strangers to become a team with a unified vision. Specifically, it concerned the organization of the business, the scope of its operations and its services. These things are soft: unlike a syringe, which is hard, they are tangible but impalpable. Soft inventions are successful only if all the people involved in their development understand and embrace the idea, with each of them making an appropriate contribution. The success of these kinds of ideas depends on more than just their suitability, feasibility and quality: a team of people with different skills needs to share a vision.

Today, innovation often means discovering how new technology fits into an organization. Like any kind of change, it is disruptive and the ramifications of the change go beyond technical issues. Back when digitizing the sales force was innovative, I worked with a client as they introduced digital sales aids on tablets to their sales force around the world. The project was developed at the company's global headquarters using extensive research and significant resources. The first countries to receive the materials were not impressed. Adoption and usage metrics were far below the desired numbers. To try to understand how the sales aids could be improved, I ran a series of Collaborative Creativity sessions, each involving participants from five or six countries. The exercises focused on identifying the customer mindset and typical objections, then constructing storyboards with an appropriate flow of medical information (using snippets of content taken directly from the unsuccessful digital sales aids). The sessions were a success: materials were finalized for the participating countries following their indications and when they were delivered they were well received and the metrics greatly improved.

The stimuli provided for the storyboards comprised pre-existing content and the storyboards the teams designed only had minimal differences from the original detail aid. So what really happened? In my opinion, the arrival of a new technology, which was centrally controlled, was perceived as a threat – a dangerous disruption of autonomy and possibly also personal prestige. The real difference was emotional: being involved and having their opinion considered was important to the participants. They needed to feel they were a part of the innovation and were able to exercise some level of control over change.

This is part of a known phenomenon called *reactance theory*. The authors of a recent study[5] explain that:

> Reactance is an unpleasant motivational arousal that emerges when people experience a threat to or loss of their free behaviors. It serves as a motivator to restore one's freedom. The amount of reactance depends on the importance of the threatened freedom and the perceived magnitude of the threat.

---

[5] C. Steindl, E. Jonas, S. Sittenthaler, E. Traut-Mattausch and J. Greenberg, 'Understanding psychological reactance: New developments and findings', *Zeitschrift für Psychologie*, 223 (4) (2015), 205–214.

I have included the previous description of a Collaborative Creativity session in this section on invention because it clearly shows how being, or not being, a part of the creation of something changes the relationship a person has with that thing. This can mean the difference between the success or failure of an idea. An element of the force of invention is the acceptance and support of an idea that derives from having contributed to the development of the idea. It also illustrates how the entity of the involvement can vary: the proverbial blank piece of paper is not always necessary to generate a co-author effect.

Collaborative Creativity engages groups of people in creative exercises because when people with different points of view share their ideas and opinions, original and interesting things emerge. In his book, *Rebel Ideas: The Power of Diverse Thinking*, Matthew Syed writes of an experiment that explored the difference between cognitively diverse and homogenous teams.

> *Those in the two groups had very different experiences of the task. Those in diverse teams found the discussion cognitively demanding. There was plenty of debate and disagreement, because different perspectives were aired. They typically came to the right decisions, but they were not wholly certain about them. The fact that they had such full and frank discussion of the case meant that they were exposed to its inherent complexity. But what of the homogenous teams? Their experiences were radically different. They found the session more agreeable because they spent most of the time, well, agreeing ... And although they were more likely to be wrong, they were far more confident about being right.[6]*

In Syed's writing, I find confirmation of my belief that cognitively demanding discussions among diverse types of people (which, by the way, involve empathy and self-discovery) help groups to understand complexity. I also believe that this 'full picture' of complexity is the key to arriving at the right decisions or new solutions (invention). It also beautifully highlights the risk of homogenous teams that aren't challenged in some way: they politely agree and fall into groupthink (which Wikipedia defines as 'a psychological phenomenon that occurs within a group of people in which the desire for harmony or conformity in the group results in an irrational or dysfunctional decision-making outcome').

---

[6] M. Syed, *Rebel Ideas: The Power of Diverse Thinking* (2019).

One of the largest and most numerically ambitious Collaborative Creativity sessions I have run was for a mature product – very mature. Like many mature products, it had a glorious past and still maintained reasonable sales; however, like an old car, years of bumps and scrapes against other, younger, brands had left it looking a bit tired. What was needed was a reinvention on a global scale, both geographical and metaphorical. This meant over 50 participants, representing nearly 30 countries, all working together. It also meant an agenda that filled two full days because of its ambitious scope.

The multinational aspect (the Americas, the European Union (EU), India, China and more) was further complicated by the client having ownership of affiliates in only half the markets; the rest were served by partnerships with independent companies and until then the commercialization of the product had been autonomously managed in each country. Furthermore, the label indications for the drug differed wildly across the many markets.

Over two days and many, many exercises, this heterogenous group was very collaborative and very creative: in 48 hours, a global brand positioning was identified and agreed upon. The surprise for all involved was that this was based on a very innovative medical education strategy. This idea seemed to come out of nowhere, but what I think really happened was that for the first time a group of experts looked at the entire picture together and by doing so saw the 'real' problem – not the one they were formally called to resolve. When this became evident, they were empowered to solve that problem, which then gave them an improved context from which to solve other problems.

The success of this Collaborative Creativity session was certainly partly due to the force of cohesion, because the methodology allowed a large and diverse group to find common ground; however, I have included it here because of the innovative outcome. Large groups that attempt to create something are often associated with the dismal outcome of design by committee. I agree that this risk exists, which is why the right setting, with appropriate tools and challenges, is needed to liberate the force of invention from large, diverse groups.

Invention can be a transformative force – after all, it has created the modern world in which we live. Collaborative Creativity always uses invention, sometimes as a means to an end and sometimes to produce new ideas. When the objective of Collaborative Creativity is innovation, what makes it distinctive is the ability to create ideas together and as a consequence of that to understand, engage with and adopt those ideas through new behaviours in a group. I believe this process of intertwined innovation and change is a fundamental part of an organization's competitive advantage in the twenty-first century. In summary, invention is like gold: it is malleable, valuable, elemental and desirable.

Realization

The force of realization is a combination of achievement, gratification, excitement and motivation, derived from exploring a problem and creating a solution in collaboration with others. Our individual happiness at work depends significantly on the self-realization we derive from the experience.

I can't say that I have ever used Collaborative Creativity where the main objective was related to realization (if someone who works in human resources would like to change that, I'd love to hear from them). I have always experienced it as a secondary product. I mentioned realization in the first example of the time-travelling doctors and it was vital in the success of the redesign of the digital sales aid (though I wasn't aware how important it was beforehand). Certainly realization has been an aspect of every Collaborative Creativity session with which I've been involved. To put it simply, people enjoy the sessions and derive a sense of achievement from the experience. This in itself is valuable, but for the positive effects to be lasting this needs to translate into something more than a day well spent. For creative work to produce persistent realization, it must be recognized as having produced a positive, tangible effect.

If work is ignored and rendered futile, its perceived value diminishes together with the satisfaction derived from performing the work. A scientific study called 'Man's Search for Meaning'[7] explored this with an experiment in which people built Lego® Bionicles in exchange for a pre-agreed sum of money. The first Bionicle the participants

---

[7] E. Kamenica and D. Prelec, 'Man's search for meaning: The case of Legos', *Journal of Economic Behavior & Organization*, 67 (2008), 671–677.

built was immediately paid the agreed sum of $3, after which the participant was given the opportunity to build another Bionicle for $2.70 and the next for $2.40 and so on until the participant declined to continue working. The experiment was designed with two different conditions of two random groups of participants. In Group 1, the completed Bionicles remained intact while the participant constructed others. In Group 2, each completed Bionicle was immediately dismantled, in full view of the participant, while they were building the next one. Basically, in Group 2 their work was rendered blatantly meaningless. The results are eloquent: in Group 1 subjects built an average of 10.6 Bionicles, while for Group 2 the average was 7.2 Bionicles – a 47.2% difference in productivity. In case you are wondering, the experiment was replicated with different types of tasks and the results were reproduced.

The conclusion I draw from this in relation to Collaborative Creativity is coherent with my personal experience: if you involve people in a creative activity – which is emotionally far more significant than constructing a toy – it is important that they believe their efforts are both useful and appreciated.

I think any company that believes their staff are an asset has a duty to listen to them and let them have some influence on the tools with which they work and the projects on which they work because people work better when they gain satisfaction from their work. It is definitely in the interest of the company to do so. The purpose and value of work are important, and self-realization is particularly vital when it comes to tasks where some level of ingenuity is required.

This means giving individuals a degree of autonomy. For this to work in an organization, it is necessary to reap the productive benefits of self-realization while also achieving organizational coherence and harmony. This means giving a group a degree of autonomy and the tools to help them collectively define how they coherently use that freedom. You need to combine self-realization with *team-realization*.

Charlie Walker-Wise is a tutor at the Royal Academy of Dramatic Art (RADA). Talking to The Economist he said, 'Acting is about finding the truth in the character and in yourself.'[8] Like an actor, people

---

[8] Bartleby, Charlie Walker-Wise, 'What businesses can learn from the arts', The Economist, 12 December 2019, www.economist.com/business/2019/12/12/what-businesses-can-learn-from-the-arts [accessed 2 June 2020].

who work for brands must deliver words and emotions that are not always their own – their job is to play a role and project a story that seldom aligns perfectly with their sense of self. Part of the job is finding the bridge between brand realization and self-realization. In Walker-Wise's words, 'The lesson from acting is how do I connect to this message without betraying my own personality.'

In a monologue, this morphing of character and actor is uninfluenced by other factors, but pharmaceutical brands have a vast cast of actors and even require audience participation. Here, actors must find the truth in both the brand and the collective.

Collaborative Creativity projects can work like the rehearsals of a stage play: everyone has a script and together the cast works out how to interpret it. Investing in this activity means that the gap between what gets planned and what gets done is narrowed and the execution is coherent. Needless to say, this approach can improve overall efficiency, both in terms of pure cost and time to completion of complex projects.

Another aspect of self-realization at work is company culture. Now, company culture isn't what you *say* it is; it's what people inside the company *think* it is, and this is informed by what they experience. Each member of staff has a slightly different experience of the organization. The day-to-day mind-fog of tasks, issues, snafus and deadlines makes it very hard to step back and gaze clearly at the over-arching reality. We all tend to see only one part of the whole.

An organization is a system, and systems work efficiently when all the components function harmoniously together. Take an automobile: it is a system for transportation made of many components, including the engine, the wheels, the brakes, the suspension, the chassis and so on. If the engine were to have consciousness, it would understand combustion but it might have no concept of roads.

In pharmaceutical companies, each of the many specialist departments that make up the whole is like a component of the automobile and tends to have a subjective, role-specific view of the business. This is normal, but it can make it difficult for the organization to be truly self-aware, able to adapt and even identify what makes it special.

Add to this the prolific activity of mergers and acquisitions in the pharmaceutical sector over the last five years and you have to wonder whether some people have any sense at all of the culture of the company that employs them. According to a 2019 GlobalData report,[9] from 2014 to the first half of 2019 there were more than 400 mergers and acquisitions in the gene therapy, immuno-oncology, microbiome and orphan drug categories alone.

Numbers are a bit cold, so take a glance at the names in the following list for the last 20 years, which includes only deals worth over $10 billion.[10] Glaxo Wellcome Plc merged with SmithKline Beecham, Amgen bought Immunex, Pfizer bought Pharmacia, Sanofi bought Aventis, Boston Scientific and Abbott Laboratories bought Guidant, Bayer bought Schering, Johnson & Johnson bought Pfizer Consumer Health, Merck Group bought Serono, AstraZeneca bought MedImmune, Schering Plough bought Organon International, Pfizer bought Wyeth, Merck & Co. bought Schering-Plough, Roche bought Genentech, Novartis bought Alcon, Sanofi bought Genzyme, Gilead Sciences bought Pharmasset, Johnson & Johnson bought Synthes, Amgen bought Onyx Pharmaceuticals, Medtronic bought Covidien, Actavis bought Forest Laboratories, Merck Group bought Sigma-Aldrich, Novartis bought GlaxoSmithKline Oncology, Bayer bought Merck & Co. Consumer Health, Zimmer Inc. bought Biomet Inc., Actavis bought Allergan, Inc., Teva Pharmaceutical Industries bought Actavis, AbbVie bought Pharmacyclics, Pfizer bought Hospira, Valeant bought Salix Pharmaceuticals, Bayer bought Monsanto, Shire bought Baxalta, Abbott Laboratories bought St Jude Medical, Boehringer Ingelheim bought Sanofi Animal Health, Johnson & Johnson bought Actelion, Gilead Sciences bought Kite Pharma, Takeda Pharmaceutical bought Shire, Sanofi bought Bioverativ, Bristol-Myers Squibb bought Celgene.

Both financially and strategically I'm sure these were all great; however, from the perspective of company culture I suspect that at least a few of them were not so great. I believe Collaborative Creativity can be used to facilitate the integration of different cultures, procedures and portfolios. Accepting change that is thrust upon us is something humans are not very good at doing. Change we can't control causes anxiety. Change we don't understand and change that

[9] GlobalData, 'Deal-making trends in pharma – thematic research' (2019), https://store.globaldata.com/report/gdhcht040--deal-making-trends-in-pharma-thematic-research [accessed 2 June 2020].
[10] Wikipedia, https://en.wikipedia.org/wiki/List_of_largest_pharmaceutical_mergers_and_acquisitions [accessed 2 June 2020].

appears to be personally negative can cause depression. When there is a perceived threat of redundancy or a loss of power (which is the inevitable concern of many employees impacted by a merger or acquisition), the willingness to collaborate and be open is impacted by the instinct to protect one's position.

To maintain morale and motivation, it is important to concede some decisions within the change to those who are affected by it. As we have already seen in the digital sales aid example, co-authorship and co-ownership of some part of change are ways to restore confidence and purpose to those who feel insecure. As we saw in the example of the mature product, change doesn't have to be fully planned and imposed: the objective can be mandated and the solution delegated. With Collaborative Creativity, change can be embraced willingly (remember that half the affiliates were different companies).

Unlike standard meetings, Collaborative Creativity sessions keep the focus on the result for the company while encouraging individual expression and realization. Their unfamiliar format (which always changes) makes it difficult for any single person to derail the exploration of a subject or manipulate it to their exclusive advantage. Gaming the system is harder if the system changes.

Realization is a joyous force – it makes people happy and proud. Collaborative Creativity always generates realization, even when uninvited, because rising to the cognitive challenge of a Collaborative Creativity session is rewarding. Beware, though, that realization is unstable. The warm glow of post-session satisfaction can easily transform into resentment and exasperation if a participant feels their efforts have been ignored. In summary, realization is like a cat: it's warm, cuddly and makes you smile, but if you don't respect it you'll soon feel its sharp claws.

Cohesion

The force of cohesion concerns ideas about a group. Belonging is an important human need. The power of cohesion resides in the things that a group shares – the things they have in common – and its effects concern the way its members function as a team. In Collaborative Creativity, this force depends greatly on empathy, as well as on the co-authorship/co-ownership of invention.

One example of cohesion was of pan-European scope. The client had a successful portfolio of drugs for a common chronic disease. It was a lucrative portfolio, but it was nearing the end of its patent and was no longer strategic for the future of the company. The leaders of the company decided to concentrate their investments in other therapeutic areas. The portfolio contained mostly mature products with one new product scheduled for launch in 14 months' time.

The decision to consolidate marketing activities in the top seven markets had been made. The objective was to maximize portfolio revenue by drastically reducing marketing spending across EU markets while maintaining current sales and ensuring the successful launch of the new product.

The marketing teams responsible for the portfolio in each country had, until now, been completely autonomous. The ways in which the products of the portfolio were promoted were entirely different in each country and even the brand name was different in certain markets. Reactions to the change from marketers in the affected countries were understandably hostile, exceptional characteristics of the local markets were brandished like weapons and predictions of doom and disaster were offered. The climate at the start of the Collaborative Creativity project, which would last three years, was sub-zero chilly.

The first Collaborative Creativity sessions helped the group to focus on and appreciate what they had in common instead of what made them different. They established that, while the change was unavoidable, how it was actuated was in fact in their hands.

The team co-created a pan-European portfolio strategy that was a first – until then, promotional efforts had been dedicated to individual products. Together, they identified types of typical customers with shared traits in the various markets and identified the tools they would co-develop to reach these customers – some of which were innovative and were possible only because the initial investment required for development was sustained by all the markets and not just one. A pan-European communication concept was developed and adopted for the portfolio and the launch of the new product. Local costs of adaptation and implementation were minimal and, by sharing the costs of development, the overall marketing spend decreased greatly over the three years while sales across the portfolio increased. The launch of the new product (the first coordinated pan-European launch for this company) was a success, which added strength to the portfolio and awareness to the broader offering of services the franchise had invented.

To achieve these goals, the first months of collaboration required many Collaborative Creativity sessions, for two reasons: first, there were a lot of things to work on; second, the team of people from different countries had to learn to work together and establish a common goal. The effects of the force of cohesion on this second point were transformational, the change in enthusiasm and energy of the group was enormous and their mutual understanding was transformed. This allowed the continuation of the project to be managed with only three or four Collaborative Creativity sessions a year.

By working together, the group made something much bigger than its members had ever done individually, and they came to appreciate that co-ownership of a big, successful and innovative project brought satisfaction and kudos superior to the solitary ownership of a single market.

Like all my examples, this one showcases many forces. Self-discovery allowed the participants to understand what was important about their role and to let go some aspects of their work in exchange for others. Realization rewarded their efforts and helped them to appreciate that the change was positive. Empathy for their customers and colleagues, together with the force of invention, allowed them to reimagine their offering as a portfolio that simplified their customers' work. In this example, though, it is the force of cohesion that is the hero: without cohesion, the other forces would have been weakened and the project would have failed.

If you aim to embrace change, it implies that you're going to be adopting a different behaviour. Sometimes this is a very conscious decision, driven by a belief – for example, 'I agree with that and I'll try to follow the suggestion.' At other times, this behaviour change may be unconscious, driven by social learning and observation. If influential people or a number of your peers start to behave in a particular way, you may simply adopt the same behaviour to remain in step. But when change is forced upon you, if you don't believe in it or you don't see any obvious role models, then it is likely that even if you are required to comply, you will merely pay lip service to the change, you will drag your feet and if you get the chance you may well revert to your previous behaviour.

The change in the relationships of the pan-European group brought about by the Collaborative Creativity sessions allowed a lot of work and decisions to be made by a heterogeneous group that initially had harboured incompatible objectives and attitudes. It also helped them establish a bond that allowed them to do a lot of collaboration remotely, with emails, file sharing and teleconferences – furthermore using English, which was not the native tongue of the majority of the team. The challenges of this should not be under-estimated.

Different modes of communication have different characteristics. We tend to find face-to-face communication easier because we are aided by many visual clues that help us comprehend the entire meaning of another person's words. Remote communication is not so rich in information but if we are well acquainted with the other person, we can imagine the tone and infer the intention.

A Collaborative Creativity session is rich in many aspects of human interaction: exchange of ideas, experience sharing, verbal communication, non-verbal communication and so on. This is the long tail of cohesion after Collaborative Creativity sessions, it makes everyday communication easier because the memory of the rich interaction of the session provides context for successive interactions. If we have lived a rich experience together and now share a collective vision and purpose, it is more likely that we will understand each other even with the bare minimum of communication.

How does a Collaborative Creativity session do this and why is it different from a standard business meeting? I think the key is the act of creativity and the dynamic created in the group. To share an idea with someone else requires a little courage, to share your creative process with someone else demands even more. Half-formed ideas, hunches, intuitions and messy half-thoughts come from deep within you, and they may easily be criticized or ridiculed. We are vulnerable when we create with others, and if the experience goes well it inspires confidence in our co-creators. When we create together, we share and inspire each other but at the same time we also build trust.

Sometimes trust isn't an issue – sometimes people are just too busy focusing on their area of competency. The client for whom I did the work with the time-travelling doctors experienced such a situation. There were many customer-facing functions within the company and they all acted a little too autonomously.

The output from the Collaborative Creativity session with physicians that I described in the introduction to the five forces was disturbing for the client: goodwill was much lower than previously believed and, with new therapies from rival companies arriving within a year, it was evident that actions needed to be taken to quickly address and mitigate the issues with the specialists. Knowing that the years of market dominance were about to end, the organization also needed to reorganize and prepare for a more competitive era.

The objective of the project was to devise a customer-centric plan that worked synergistically across all customer-facing internal functions. This was a significant challenge because at the time the functions were extremely autonomous and uncoordinated.

I prepared Collaborative Creativity sessions that involved representatives of the relevant internal functions: marketing, medical, digital, market access and public affairs. The scope of these sessions was to help the group achieve full comprehension of the output of the healthcare professional Collaborative Creativity session, to reflect on its significance for the brand and to examine possible counter-measures within the strategic framework mandated by the company's headquarters.

The group successfully developed a comprehensive and realistic profile of the customer. It devised a series of responses aimed at resolving the physician's issues and produced a coordinated plan (in a storyboard format) that ensured the sequence of all collective actions and messages was coherent. The group also worked on ways to stay synchronized in the future.

With just four Collaborative Creativity sessions (one with customers and three involving internal staff), the client had upgraded their customer comprehension and empathy, and devised a coherent response that was rapidly executed.

Obviously, I can't know what would have happened if the above actions had not been taken, but I am convinced that the competitors would have found a far more receptive market than they did. Despite the arrival of two strong rival therapies that inevitably diluted the client's share of sales, they never lost leadership in the category.

Collaborative Creativity can also be used as an ongoing, periodic exercise to improve unity of purpose and the focus of corporate teams. A Collaborative Creativity retreat, for example, is a quarterly off-site gathering, where a group can detach from day-to-day obligations and reflect collectively, ponder things that are important but not urgent, explore the future and expand the group's consciousness regarding the possible implications of changes and current issues. Gazing into the future and ruminating on the present might seem a luxury for all but the highest-ranking individuals in an organization, but I believe the benefits of these kinds of activities greatly outweigh the investment.

Each retreat has different creative exercises, and the topics on which it focuses are chosen partly by the leadership and partly by the rest of the team. In this way, each can highlight things that concern or interest them and explore them without a specific project or work stream having been initiated. Performed regularly – once every quarter or at least every six months – they can contribute to the collective consciousness and overall performance of a team.

Cohesion is a fragile force. It requires constant attention because when neglected it dissipates. Without cohesion, every collective endeavour is more difficult and less likely to produce extraordinary results. Cohesion is relatively easy to generate: it is a secondary product of every Collaborative Creativity session and there is no downside to cohesion. In summary, cohesion is like a coffee machine: it brings people together, facilitates rapport and energizes them, but it must be maintained or it will stop working.

Five-in-one

In this chapter, I have presented the five forces of Collaborative Creativity using examples of sessions I devised and moderated. Before we move on, I want to briefly explain that my observations don't derive only from my role as a designer and organizer, but are heavily informed by the perspective of the participant.

My career began in 1983 as a creative in an advertising agency. I was an art director, responsible for creating ads with a copywriter partner. Together we would co-create dozens of concepts for each assignment and develop the best idea together – with the copywriter being responsible for the words and the art director responsible for the visual aspect.

At work, I lived with the forces of self-discovery, empathy, invention, realization and cohesion. I didn't call them that at the time, and

I didn't consciously acknowledge their existence or analyse their effects and interactions, but in a pragmatic way I was aware of them and how they functioned and influenced the quality of my work. When I became a creative director, responsible for how others generated ideas and collaborated creatively, I started to become more consciously aware of these forces and their dynamics.

Then at a certain point I began working with American agencies that devised global work by inviting creatives from around the world to physically attend a live event called a Creative Wave (sometimes called a Creative Rave). These gatherings lasted days, usually involved between 20 and 40 creatives and were dedicated exclusively to intense creativity. I was impressed by the format, the quality of the work and the immediacy with which complete strangers from different cultures quickly bonded and became productive. I was surprised by how the ownership of the work was shared and how freely other people's ideas were adapted, repurposed and enhanced. I participated in a lot of these events and ended up running many of them myself.

At a certain point, the agencies started inviting clients to work with the creatives. That was when I fully comprehended that the forces of Collaborative Creativity were universal. I understood that guiding unexperienced people in creative exercises allowed them to express themselves effectively and joyfully. I experienced how when very different people with diverse experience work together, their unusual chemistry helps them to produce unusual, original ideas.

I saw that the experience of creating something with someone else – which I had enjoyed for years as the by-product of making advertising – was powerful and useful in and of itself with many potential applications. Eventually, I even realized that, in certain circumstances, the effects of producing the ideas were more valuable than the ideas themselves.

What happens in a Collaborative Creativity session is complex; many things coexist and many feelings and actions are intertwined. Some of the consequences of group creativity can be planned, while others just happen unsummoned and unannounced. The five forces of Collaborative Creativity are a convenient way of describing the things that I have consistently observed happening in group creativity. They are a construct that helps me (and hopefully you) to understand the effects of Collaborative Creativity.

Figure 2 explains the relationships I believe exist between the forces.

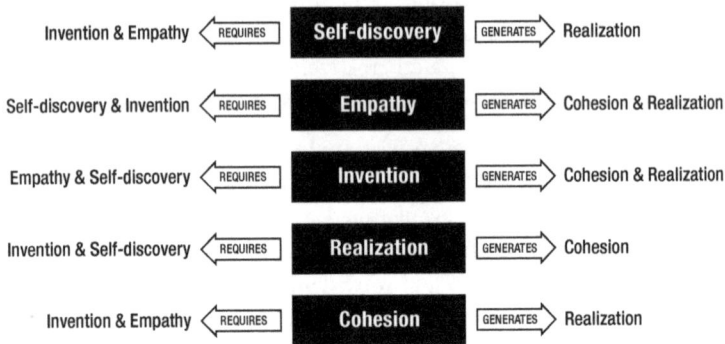

Invention & Empathy ⟨REQUIRES	**Self-discovery**	GENERATES⟩ Realization
Self-discovery & Invention ⟨REQUIRES	**Empathy**	GENERATES⟩ Cohesion & Realization
Empathy & Self-discovery ⟨REQUIRES	**Invention**	GENERATES⟩ Cohesion & Realization
Invention & Self-discovery ⟨REQUIRES	**Realization**	GENERATES⟩ Cohesion
Invention & Empathy ⟨REQUIRES	**Cohesion**	GENERATES⟩ Realization

Figure 2: Relationships between the forces of Collaborative Creativity

Looking at Figure 2, you can see at a glance that if, for example, you want to use Collaborative Creativity to produce cohesion in a group, you will need to design exercises that focus on invention and empathy. If you want to produce empathy in a group, you will need to design exercises that focus on self-discovery and invention.

Figure 2 illustrates how the forces are dependent upon each other and are in fact five-in-one. This isn't because I made it so; it is because the five forces construct represents human behaviours – our actions and reactions in the field of Collaborative Creativity.

In this chapter, I have presented examples of different applications of Collaborative Creativity. Each was chosen because it was particularly effective at highlighting the power of a certain force. I have also been careful to mention other forces in play because the forces of Collaborative Creativity always coexist, although their relative strengths vary in each situation.

In the real world, companies don't ask for cohesion; they ask for collaboration between functions, operational efficiency and employee performance improvements. Figure 3 connects practical applications with the effects of the five forces and the forces themselves. Obviously, there are numerous needs and the figure can only contain a few examples, so this is an incomplete list of possible applications; nonetheless, I think it is useful for connecting theory and practical application. My aim here is only to suggest how the five forces can be pragmatically useful. For a more detailed account of how to apply the forces of Collaborative Creativity to a specific problem or need, read on to Part 2 of this book.

APPLICATION	EFFECT OF FORCE	FORCE
Market research	Uncover subconscious beliefs	Self-discovery
Change management		
Customer-centric projects	Understand emotions	
Team harmony and collaboration		
Mission development	Comprehend shared values in a group	
Team building + motivation		
User experience design	Transfer personal experiences	Empathy
Education		
Service development	Understand the point of view of others	
Collaboration between functions/organizations		
Patient support service design	Comprehend the emotions of others	
Brand communication		
Innovation of brand offering	Generate product/service ideas	Invention
Future-proofing of brand offering		
Mergers and other hierarchy disruption	Generate organisational ideas	
Operational innovation		
User-generated comms ideas	Generate communication ideas	
Global strategy and localization		
Customer experience	Satisfaction	Realization
Employee experience		
Innovation development	Co-authorship/ownership	
Change management		
Employee performance improvement	Motivation	
Team building + motivation		
Collaboration between functions/organisations	Alignment	Cohesion
Operational efficiency		
Company culture	Belonging	
Team building + motivation		
Employee performance improvement	Pride	
Employee experience		

Figure 3: Practical applications and effects of the five forces

But before we move on to the how-to section of this book, which explains how to design and run Collaborative Creativity sessions in practical situations, it is useful to examine a few more things related to overall context.

Making sense

Recent discoveries in cognitive neuroscience, behavioural economics and psychology have revealed to us that human behaviour is not rational, fully conscious and logical; to the contrary, we are emotional, illogical, self-deceptive and impulsive beings.

David Eagleman writes that, 'The conscious mind is not at the centre of the action in the brain; instead, it is far out on a distant edge, hearing but whispers of the activity.'[11] Eagleman tells us that the vast majority of brain activity is non-conscious and the things we call instincts, habits, preferences, perceptions and desires are the result of neural sub-routines – independent of conscious thought. He proposes that the role of consciousness is to manage an increasing number of complex and competing neural sub-routines.

Daniel Kahneman[12] famously calls the conscious-unconscious modes 'System 1 thinking' (fast, automatic, frequent, emotional, stereotypic, unconscious) and 'System 2 thinking' (low, effortful, infrequent, logical, calculating, conscious). Kahneman tells us that we have two selves: the *experiencing self* (System 1 thinking) and the *remembering self* (System 2 thinking). The experiencing self lives in and understands only the present moment; the remembering self

---

[11] D. Eagleman, *Incognito: The Secret Lives of the Brain* (2011), 9.

[12] D. Kahneman, *Thinking, Fast and Slow* (2011).

catalogues stories (memories) and influences our future actions by proposing anticipated stories (future memories).

Robert Trivers[13] argues that natural selection has favoured self-deception because it makes us more convincing liars and the ability to fool others provides an advantage for survival and procreation.

In summary, some of the best minds of our age think that: much of our brain's activity is 'mindless'; we fixate on stories rather than facts; and we are all self-deceiving mythomaniacs.

Collaborative Creativity uses the creative act as a way to bridge the divide between conscious and unconscious. Sharing stories, memories and experience, and creating new stories, are at the heart of Collaborative Creativity exercises because ultimately the things we remember (both good and bad) are the things we care about and the things we create are echoes of future memories. Collaborative Creativity employs role-playing, third-person storytelling, free association and numerous other techniques to side-step deceit and self-deception.

If we accept the ideas of Eagleman, Kahneman and Trivers, we are forced to conclude that approaches such as Collaborative Creativity are needed in business. It makes no sense to continue to operate exclusively with logical rigour when the evidence indicates that a large part of human behaviour ignores facts and logic.

To a great extent, experience is a product of expectation. In other words, our memories of past experiences influence and modify present experiences. Consider, for example, your favourite dish that your mother has always made for you since you were a child. Nobody else has ever made that particular dish quite like your mother, right? I can assure you that nobody ever will. That dish is special not because of organoleptic characteristics: it is special because of psychological characteristics and memory. The expectation you have of tasting your favourite mum-made dish primes your senses and actually changes your whole experience. It tastes different because you expect it to taste different, because you want it to taste different. If you take away the knowledge that your mother made that dish, the food she has prepared loses all added value and consequently its special taste. The following is a famous example of this phenomenon with a brand.

---

[13] R. Trivers, *The Folly of Fools: The Logic of Deceit and Self-Deception in Human Life* (2011).

In 1985, the Coca-Cola Company announced a change to its formula introducing a 'smoother, sweeter taste'. Coca-Cola was the number one cola manufacturer at the time, but Pepsi had continually gained market share in the previous 15 consecutive years as the two brands fought an intense marketing war. One weapon used by Pepsi was the 'Pepsi Challenge'. This consisted of a blind taste test between the two drinks that revealed a slight preference for the taste of Pepsi. Spooked market researchers working for Coca-Cola did their own taste tests with nearly 200,000 consumers and identified a new Coca-Cola formula that beat Pepsi in blind tests. The New Coke launched on 23 April 1985 with advertising that boasted 'The Best Just Got Better!'

This was all very logical and scientific: the data said the majority of people would prefer the new taste. The consumer reaction was huge and quite the opposite of what Coca-Cola were expecting. People were outraged and grassroots campaigns sprung up across the country demanding that Coca-Cola bring back the original Coke. On 11 July 1985, Donald Keough, the then President of Coca-Cola, held a press conference to officially announce the return of the old Coke formula and apologize: 'The simple fact is that all of the time and money and skill poured into consumer research on a new Coca-Cola could not measure or reveal the depth and abiding emotional attachment to original Coca-Cola felt by so many people.'

At the time, the New Coke debacle was attributed to the fact that people don't like change, but 19 years later details of a study appeared in *Neuron* magazine.[14] In the study, researchers used functional magnetic resonance imaging (fMRI) to measure brain activity levels while conducting their own taste tests with Coca-Cola and Pepsi. The fMRI allowed the researchers to discover the specific brain regions activated in response to subjects tasting the drinks. The experiments used blind testing (where subjects didn't know what they were drinking) and branded testing (where subjects knew whether they were drinking Coca-Cola or Pepsi before they drank it).

As expected, in all the blind tests the brain systems known to be involved in taste were seen to be activated and the same occurred when the subjects knew they were drinking Pepsi. Something very different

---

[14] S. M. McClure, J. Li, D. Tomlin, K. S. Cypert, L. M. Montague and P. R. Montague, 'Neural correlates of behavioral preference for culturally familiar drinks', *Neuron*, 44 (2) (2004), 379–387.

happened when subjects knew they were drinking Coca-Cola – in these cases, the dorsolateral prefrontal cortex and the hippocampus were also activated (both are implicated in emotion-based behaviour modification). The experience of drinking Coca-Cola was seen by fMRI to be composed of more than just the information from the subjects' taste buds. Expectation, based on previously experienced emotions, changed the subjects' experience of reality.

In the world of pharmaceuticals, the prime example of expectation-modifying experience is, of course, the placebo effect – which is also, perhaps more accurately, called the 'expectation effect'. The following is taken from a study published in 2015:

> What we believe we will experience from a treatment – our expectation – has a substantial impact on what we actually experience. Expectation has been established as a key process behind the placebo effect. Studies in both laboratory and clinical settings consistently show that when people ingest a pharmacologically inert substance (placebo) but believe that it is an active substance, they experience both the subjective sensations and physiologic effects expected from that active substance. Expectation has an important place in the response to 'real' treatment as well. This paper provides an overview of the data which point to the role of expectation in both the placebo effect and the response to treatment. These data suggest that clinicians might enhance the benefit of all treatments by promoting patients' positive expectations.[15]

Reality is subjective – each of us creates our own sense of the world, and this is only partly based on what our senses capture; it is also influenced by what our minds expect, hope and believe.

Pharmaceutical companies are founded on science – chemistry and biology – where hard facts and data rule. Today, advances in personal technology mean there is more data available on individual behaviour and health than ever before. It is exciting that patterns and trends that previously were invisible can be detected by machine learning. But what of the correct interpretation of that data? How do we uncover the beliefs or unconscious behaviours that are producing the data? If we use logic to try to devise an explanation, we risk attributing a fallacious logical behaviour to something without logic, something driven by emotion.

---

[15] W. A. Brown, 'Expectation, the placebo effect and the response to treatment', *Rhode Island Medical Journal*, 98 (5) (2013), 19–21.

In a recent study by Forrester Consulting, sponsored by FocusVision,[16] only 23% of the survey participants – all from large organizations (1,000-plus employees) across the globe – said they believed their organization understood why its customers acted the way they did, despite access to a wealth of customer data.

And what of the risk of inherent bias in data collection? Catherine D'Ignazio, an Assistant Professor of Urban Science and Planning in the Department of Urban Studies and Planning at MIT, said in a recent interview with *The Guardian* that:

> There is a naive assumption that if you see numbers in a spreadsheet, they are real somehow. But data is never this raw, truthful input, and it is never neutral. It is information that has been collected in certain ways by certain actors and institutions for certain reasons.[17]

Then there is the issue of what isn't measured. Something we don't or can't measure is not necessarily devoid of value; equally, something we don't fully comprehend is not devoid of influence.

James Harding, editor and co-founder of *Tortoise*, recently wrote in relation to journalism that, 'There is a seam of life that the news finds particularly hard to cover: it's not what people do or what people say, but how we feel. It's impossible to quantify, of course, or double-source.'[18]

Even if, in a hypothetical world, data were complete and unbiased and business was conducted entirely with 'System 2 thinking', it would still need a way to understand and engage the rest of the world, which functions mostly with 'System 1 thinking'. I recognize the importance of data and agree with those who think it will become increasingly pervasive and accurate. I refute the idea that regarding

---

[16] Forrester Consulting, *How Customers Think, Feel, and Act: The Paradigm of Business Outcomes* (Forrester Consulting, sponsored by FocusVision, 2019), https://cloud. kapostcontent.net/pub/d2a85d5e-c053-4bfc-ae8d-f1a9c0b2af31/whitepaper-how-customers-think-feel-and-act-the-paradigm-of-business-outcomes?kui=M tTZamfFfmzvSS4fnSaD4Q [accessed 2 June 2020].

[17] Z. Corbyn, 'Catherine D'Ignazio: Data is never a raw truthful input – and it is never neutral', *The Guardian*, 21 March, www.theguardian.com/technology/2020/mar/21/catherine-dignazio-data-is-never-a-raw-truthful-input-and-it-is-never-neutral [accessed 2 June 2020].

[18] J. Harding, 'This week in *Tortoise*: Pressure and pressure valves', 27 April 2020.

human behaviour data can tell us everything and that decisions based exclusively on data and logic are infallible.

The world of healthcare is human-centric, with people working to help people who are sick. To design better healthcare solutions, I think more of that work should be applied to how we examine and accommodate the emotional, irrational and duplicitous reality of human nature.

Exceptional pharma

The pharmaceuticals sector is a highly specialized world, as Brian D. Smith writes: 'No other industry is so far from typical along so many dimensions. The life sciences industry really is exceptional.'[19]

Just consider the market complexity of pharmaceuticals. In most cases, the customer – the person who makes the product decision – is not the end user and not the purchaser. The decision is influenced by scientific literature and guidelines, but also by local rules and formulae – and, of course, the personal clinical experience of the customer. Even the customer's personal experience is actually second-hand: they prescribe a treatment but, apart from hospitalized patients, they can't know whether their prescription is actually adhered to. The presence of adverse effects, comorbidities, drug–drug interactions, food–drug interactions and the need to manage complex treatment regimes are also factors that contribute to product choice. Patient advocacy groups and caregivers can influence the end user and the customer in various ways and the product decision is often affected to some degree by other professional caregivers, healthcare managers and regulators. With all that going on, and more, it can be incredibly challenging to understand what actually affects prescription choice. With such a rich customer and stakeholder ecosystem, attempts at being customer-centric can be mind boggling

---

[19] Brian D. Smith, *Leadership in the Life Sciences: Ten Lessons from the C-Suite of Pharmaceutical and Medical Technology Companies* (2019).

and some may even consider it futile. While recognizing that it is mind boggling, I disagree that it is futile. I think anything that can contribute to understanding the decisions and behaviours in play is potentially useful.

The end user (the patient or caregiver) has traditionally been off-limits for communication regarding prescription drugs, with the United States and New Zealand being the only exceptions to this rule. However, the intention of keeping medical information confined to the professional class has been thwarted by the Internet. Two decades of access to Google have made the average patient both more informed and misinformed than ever before. The role of patient advocacy groups and expert patients – people with a long-term health condition who, by understanding and managing their condition, are able to assume greater control over their health and gain benefits in terms of quality of life – as sources of unbiased and reliable information is increasingly important. There are growing signs of institutions and government now listening to the perspectives of those who live with healthcare issues. Much remains to be done to help close the information loop and ensure therapies are understood and correctly adhered to by patients.

Another defining aspect of the pharmaceutical industry is that the vast majority of new products are driven by science not the market, which means that most new treatments are what science is currently able to offer, not necessarily what the market actually wants or needs. Even if it were possible to develop treatments at will, based on market needs, the time currently required to develop, test and commercialize a drug is so lengthy that by the time a treatment is launched, the market for which it was designed could have changed radically. Furthermore, marketers are not free to say what they wish about their brands, as the claims that can be made about a product are defined by the results of clinical trials and other scientific literature.

This leads us to a defining aspect of the pharmaceutical industry: regulation. Because competition between pharmaceutical brands and corporations ultimately relates to human illness and suffering, the industry is highly regulated. This external regulation has led pharmaceutical companies to structure their internal organization in an effort to ensure that checks and balances enforce external and internal regulation and pre-empt any abuses or irregularities. Within any typical pharmaceutical company, there are daily internal battles between different functions, each striving to fulfil their contrasting roles. This tension is necessary but can become excessive and even undermine the common goal of delivering treatments to as many people as can benefit from them.

I think it is fair to say that the environment in which pharmaceutical companies operate is exceptional and the way they are organized reflects this, but in the end there is one thing that pharma shares with every other type of company and that is people.

Karenann Terrell, Chief Digital Officer at GlaxoSmithKline, put it succinctly: 'Patients are consumers who got sick.'[20] Her point is that the changes that a person sees in society become a norm that creates a general expectation. For example, we have become accustomed to sending text messages to communicate with the company that supplies electricity to our home, and to brands responding promptly with information when it is requested through email or Twitter, so when that response doesn't occur we find it odd or rude. The expectations of service created by consumer brands have become the standard expected from everything – including healthcare.

Today, a typical patient is a more enlightened end user than in the past. The Internet has allowed the majority of people to evolve from a passive and accepting attitude towards healthcare professionals to a more proactive and demanding stance. An increasing number of patients are influencers and patient advocacy groups, social media and specific chat groups have become public spaces where people share or seek the experiences and opinions of others with the same condition.

If patients are consumers who got sick, physicians are consumers who make a living curing the sick. Doctors are highly skilled, trained professionals but that doesn't make them robots: they are people. Let's look at a fictitious but credible head of an oncology department, sitting at their desk: on their wrist is a Rolex watch, in their right hand is a Montblanc pen and in their pocket rests the key to a Mercedes. These brand choices are not rational: they are not driven by data and cold logic – they are all about feeling good. The same

---

[20] Words spoken during a panel discussion at the HLTH event in Las Vegas, 28 October 2019 and reported by Marc Iskowitz, www.mmm-online.com/home/channel/pharma-trying-to-transform-itself-but-must-get-out-of-its-own-way-first-says-novartis-digital-chief [accessed 2 June 2020].

impulses and needs that influence their choice of watch are also in play, to some degree, in work decisions.

Many types of behaviour in healthcare are hard or impossible to observe, so the only source of information is what people will tell us, and what people tell us is, at best, what they tell themselves. Unfortunately this does not always coincide with the truth, the whole truth and nothing but the truth. The complexity of the healthcare world is also the complexity of humans and their interactions and relationships. The more we can learn about this and the more we can empower people to understand and be understood by others, the better — for overall care, for access and diagnosis, for adherence and for health outcomes.

Creativity and ideas

Creativity begins with dissatisfaction with something, which provokes a desire to change it; this leads to ideas about how to make the change and finally action that creates the change. Within an individual, this sequence occurs in a self-regulating way. Within organizations, creativity requires the right conditions for it to flow and for its ideas to flourish.

Moving chronologically, it all starts with dissatisfaction – an issue, a problem. This is not as straightforward as it might seem at first glance. Consider the example I described previously of the digital sales aid. The dissatisfaction that initiated everything was with the initial adoption and usage metrics of the digital tool. The problem causing this was identified in the way the content was designed because it was heavily and widely criticized. As we saw, though, the real problem was the emotional reaction of the local marketers and sales people to the new tool. Fortunately, local marketers were involved in the redesign of the content but, with the information we had at the time, we could just as easily and justifiably have decided to involve relevant healthcare professionals instead. After the first Collaborative Creativity session, where we understood the real issue, we made sure to also include field force area managers in the following sessions. The problem wasn't a redesign: it was change. The redesign became an opportunity to obtain acceptance of change.

The point is that even the most brilliant creativity will ultimately fail if it is *solving the wrong issue*. Fixing the wrong problem is like curing a symptom without understanding and addressing the underlying cause. Time spent identifying the root cause of a problem is time well spent.

Dissatisfaction (together with opportunity) is at the heart of revolutionary innovation, also known as disruption. Most of the time, we simply accept the status quo and we adapt to accommodate inconvenient things – we tend to devise work-arounds rather than invent solutions. Whether this is lazy or efficient depends on the situation. For us to consciously feel the need for something to improve, it must generate a certain level of dissatisfaction. For us to actively be driven to radically change something, we must be extremely dissatisfied.

'If I had asked people what they wanted, they would have said faster horses.' This famous quote has been attributed to Henry Ford by Jean-Marie Dru, Chairman of TBWA Worldwide.[21] There is truth in the phrase, regardless of who said it. At the time, horses were the most common form of personal transport and people accepted them; they weren't really that dissatisfied. Incremental improvement is the result of minor dissatisfaction while true innovation is the result of chronic dissatisfaction and the ability to look beyond the perceived problem to the actual need. Would you like a better horse or do you need a better mode of transportation? These are the kinds of questions that should be answered before you ask people to start having ideas.

Which leads us to the desire to change something. This is the part where we frame the problem. The way a creative process is designed has a significant impact on the output. I am convinced that only 50% of creative thinking is actually original problem solving; the other 50% is framing and asking the right questions. The best thinkers are people who ask interesting questions and through them find surprising answers. When you are faced with a problem, you are likely to express it as a question. This is what we can call the Big Question.

Trying to solve the Big Question head-on rarely leads to interesting or truly novel ideas unless, of course, the Big Question is unique and very unusual, which is uncommon. So a way forward is to ask different questions – sub-questions that are related, but slightly

---

[21] Jean-Marie Dru, *Beyond Disruption: Changing the Rules in the Marketplace* (2002).

tangential, to the Big Question. These sub-questions relate to components of the overarching problem. By questioning assumptions about the components of the problem, it is possible to find novel solutions. The more unusual the sub-question, the more unusual the ideas it will provoke. In practice, the best ideas always seem to arrive from the 'right' sub-question – one that opens an interesting avenue of thought or exposes a weakness in previous assumptions.

A client of mine wanted to make a smart phone app to help a certain type of clinician, so I organized a Collaborative Creativity session with a dozen doctors. The Big Question was: What kind of new app would be most useful in your clinical practice?

As usual, I designed the session to include various exercises, some of which tackled the question head-on, while others addressed sub-questions. One exercise asked the following sub-question: What would you like to eliminate from your practice?

This produced a list of dissatisfactions and a couple of these sparked a conversation about an app that could simplify a small part of the clinician's workload. The client ended up producing two apps, one that originated from the 'something new' question and the other from the 'elimination' question. The utilization metrics of the app that originated from the elimination question were much higher than those of the other app.

People who pursue a creative career develop the ability to deconstruct problems, identify the components and play with questions because ideas are the answers to questions. If you spend time observing the creative process in a group setting, by far the most frequently used snippets of conversation you will hear are, 'What if...?', 'Why not...?', 'Could we...?' and 'What about...?' It is revealing that, in a creative environment, even ideas are presented as questions.

Now, when people who aren't usually creative are called upon to produce ideas, the responsibility for the questions falls to whoever designs the creative challenges because these influence the way the problem will be approached. It is important to appreciate this and design the creative challenge thoughtfully, as the way a problem is framed by creative exercises influences the ideas it generates.

Another thing that influences the ideas produced is the risk associated with them. Let me explain through a personal example from when I was an art director. The pressure to have great ideas was always intense, both for the benefit of the client and the agency for which I worked, but also for my career – agencies hire people with great work in their portfolio. Equally strong was the pressure to execute work brilliantly, on time and on budget. The result of this was that I self-censored some (potentially great) ideas because I thought the personal risk associated with their execution was too high. When I participated in the Creative Waves I have described previously, the only responsibility I had was to have great ideas. I knew that the execution of any idea that went forward was someone else's responsibility. My idea production was filterless.

In start-up culture, 'fail-fast' is a popular philosophy, and recently the idea of accepting failure appears to have become more mainstream. Psychologically, though, failure is always a negative experience and one we unconsciously try to avoid. When designing a creative challenge, to achieve the best results the desire for change must always be greater than the risk of failure.

All fired up with dissatisfaction and the desire to change? Now all you need are ideas. So perhaps it is time to brainstorm. I wouldn't if I were you. A brainstorm is a meeting, and meetings are not creative environments.

How many meetings have you been in where different people have proposed different ideas and the meeting has effectively degenerated into a battle of personalities and egos because the argument was ostensibly about the ideas but ultimately was predominantly about power, status and personal agendas? I've seen too many, and none of them were productive. Even if something is achieved, and some kind of agreement is reached on an idea, it is in the guise of an uneasy truce that leaves in its wake friction and possibly even small acts of sabotage.

Unfortunately, human understanding is 'state-dependent'. If we are in an aggressive or defensive state (which easily occurs when protecting an idea), we become argumentative and our ability to comprehend our 'opponent' is greatly diminished, precisely because we identify them in this way. When we listen to them, we are attentive only for weaknesses in their argument, so we don't try to understand their point of view. Ultimate proof of this is when we interrupt and actually talk over the other person – we literally don't want to hear what they have to say. There are other, more subtle, passive-aggressive forms of non-listening too. The most common one is when you catch yourself doing something else – checking and responding to phone messages, for example – while the other person is talking. These and other non-collaborative modes are toxic for creativity.

The first thing to do is completely separate the production of ideas and the judgement of those ideas. Creativity lives in the realm of infinite possibility. Critical thought is the opposite: it eliminates possibilities. Keep the two apart – there is a time and place for creating and a time and place for judgement, this separation is conducive to making people comfortable and confident. Providing the right environment is a fundamental aspect of group creativity, which we will examine in more detail later.

Motivating people to create is equally important. The motivation can come from higher purpose, ambition, duty or even our old friend: risk of failure. In this case, the risk of failure is of not producing any ideas. When a positive atmosphere is created, social pressure makes the idea of not having an idea to share scarier than having to share an idea with others.

The people we tend to identify as creative have the self-confidence to share their ideas with others, habitually surround themselves with interesting stimuli and have developed an ability to quickly put themselves in other people's shoes. Another characteristic of these people is the ability to solve problems, and the good news is that everybody has that ability to some degree. So, starting from their innate ability to solve problems, what else can we do to help someone have ideas?

A lack of confidence in one's ideas inhibits the ability to share them with others, which is a serious obstacle to creativity. People who don't identify as creative are often victims of their 'inner critic', a common, self-defeating psychological trait that can be amplified in intimidating environments. Fortunately, the inner critic can be silenced – at least temporarily – in the right setting.

Ultimately, giving people permission to be creative and helping them to believe they are the right choice to tackle a certain problem is the simplest thing you can do to encourage ideas. After all, if you've invited these people to produce ideas you must have had a valid reason for including them. That reason makes them an expert. Tell them up front why the group was selected and why solving the problem at hand matters, why it makes a difference.

In a professional creative environment, supplying interesting stimuli is the responsibility of the designer of the creative exercise. Stimuli are very influential on the output. People are good at recognizing patterns and discerning the logic of things, so it's a good idea to throw in some completely random stuff together with your carefully selected stimuli. If you are looking for originality, a dash of incongruous stimuli can stimulate the production of unusual ideas.

Seeing a problem from someone else's perspective is important for creativity. This can be achieved through appropriate stimuli, but whenever possible, the best way is to create mixed groups with people of relevant but diverse experiences. The collaboration of diverse minds in producing ideas allows ideas to represent different points of view and usually leads to a broader range of ideas.

That last point is a very important one. People who aren't used to producing ideas are typically more productive when they can work with others. Bouncing ideas off people is stimulating, enjoyable and has the crucial characteristic of moving thoughts in unexpected directions.

Presuming all has gone well so far: you now have some ideas. Before they become actions, though, there is much to watch out for. Ideas are susceptible to laws similar to those of natural selection. The most able to adapt are the most likely to survive. Some ideas are immutable: they have a monolithic quality. For these ideas to be successful, they must correspond perfectly to their environment, which means being compatible with the mindset of their intended recipients. A different breed of ideas is adaptable ideas, which have certain distinctive traits but also other aspects that are variable. Such ideas can adapt to different environments and allow personalization by their intended recipients or designated intermediaries.

This book is an example of a monolithic idea. The thoughts it contains, the style in which it is written, the organization and exposition of the content are all immutable. The subject of the book, Collaborative Creativity, is an adaptable idea. It has defining principles and characteristics that make it distinctive but it is extremely flexible and actually demands personalization. The book can only be read, while the idea of Collaborative Creativity can be adopted in your personal, individual way.

If you have more than one good idea, selecting the idea with which to move forward can be hard. If your aim is originality, it is best that one person or a very small group makes the decision. Every idea needs leadership to provide direction and steer it away from the bland banality that is often the result of group decision-making. However, when making decisions, that leadership must be in tune with the mindset of the intended recipients of the idea. We all have cognitive biases and personal interests, which inevitably make each reaction we have to an idea completely subjective. Without true empathy for the intended recipients, we can't go beyond our personal taste and preferences. It's like choosing a present for someone: the aim isn't to find something *you* like, it's to find something the *recipient* will like.

Sometimes you just have to present ideas to an individual or a group of people for them to select and approve development. Unless you can control the presentation (and have enough time to explain who the idea is for and demonstrate why it is valid), this is one of the riskiest moments for an idea. Again, for the idea to be understood you must make efforts to help decision-makers identify with the mindset of the intended recipients of the idea.

Before an idea can go into the world, it needs to be developed. If group creativity is great for producing ideas, it is perfect for developing them. The greater the number and diversity of the people who contribute to an idea, the stronger the idea's chances of success – both because diverse contributions can improve it and because the more friends an idea has, the better.

Fortunately, most people are happy to contribute to an idea if given the space and permission to do so. This is worthwhile because if an idea is co-created by many, by default it is also co-owned, and co-ownership translates into more people having an interest in the success of an idea and consequently its chances of success. There is even a cognitive bias, called the IKEA effect, that supports this.[22] The IKEA effect describes the fact that people give higher value to things they have had a role in creating. As the name implies, it states that even if the role is objectively small, it is subjectively perceived to be disproportionately significant. Assembling a piece of prefabricated furniture isn't the height of creativity, but as it turns out, that doesn't matter at all. Having a role in the realization of something is far more significant than the relative importance of that role.

---

[22] M. I. Norton, D. Mochon and D. Ariely, 'The IKEA effect: When labor leads to love', *Journal of Consumer Psychology*, 22 (2012), 453–460.

In many organizations, there is a tendency to assign a small group to work on a new idea in isolation, defining the finest details until they are ready for their finalized project to be launched. Then they either attempt to obtain consensus, or 'buy in', from the rest of the organization to bring it to full fruition or, in command and control structures, they simply 'roll out' (an apt term because it is reminiscent of a steamroller) the new deal.

In either case, as the idea is propagated, the *not-invented-here syndrome* kicks in, rather like an auto-immune response. The not-invented-here syndrome stifles thousands of otherwise healthy ideas every year; it is another manifestation of reactance theory (I have mentioned this previously – it is the human tendency to resist change and resent any threat to one's sense of agency).

All successful corporations are staffed with clever, competent and competitive people. Within a team, being competitive is a double-edged sword; it can be useful in the creative process but it can also be detrimental, especially when selecting, developing and adopting ideas, because competition and collaboration are like oil and water. Competition and self-interest are detrimental to creative collaboration unless they are mitigated by co-ownership.

The success of any idea is dependent on its execution. I think it is self-evident that an idea that is poorly or unevenly executed will never reach its true potential and in large organizations great execution requires collaboration and, in my opinion, co-ownership. In conclusion, I will repeat what I have said before: the more friends an idea has, the better, because successful ideas are accepted and adopted.

2 How to use Collaborative Creativity

Do-it-yourself

The first section of this book focused on what you can do with Collaborative Creativity and why it is useful. This section is all about how to do it – or, to be more precise, it describes how I do it. One of the core tenets of Collaborative Creativity is customization: it is personalized for each situation to achieve the best possible outcome. Consequently, there is a framework but no standard agenda or standard exercises. This gives you freedom to apply the method in any way you see fit, making it your own, adapting it to solve the problems you face and reaching your objectives. Not only can you create your own exercises, but you can incorporate into Collaborative Creativity sessions exercises that derive from other methods. As long as they are functional to the objective of the session and fit well with the other exercises, there is absolutely no problem with that.

You'll see that I talk of the 'client' and the 'coach'. A client is the organization and the people within that organization who commission (or sponsor) a Collaborative Creativity project to solve a problem. A coach is a person who designs a Collaborative Creativity project and is responsible for its execution. I use these terms because it makes it easy to understand the respective roles and also because my experience has always been working as a coach for a client. Obviously, this does not preclude the use of Collaborative Creativity by the employees of a pharmaceutical company without involving an external party – and in fact I encourage this. In those situations, however, I would recommend the designation of two different colleagues in the roles of client and coach because I think it beneficial to the project that the responsibilities of these roles remain separated.

With the intent of simplifying the explanation of the Collaborative Creativity method, I have provided separate explanations of the Collaborative Creativity project, the Collaborative Creativity session and the Collaborative Creativity exercise. Please don't let this deceive you into thinking these are autonomous elements: they are the vital and interconnected components of a single system.

Figure 4 illustrates the structure and relationship of the three main components of Collaborative Creativity.

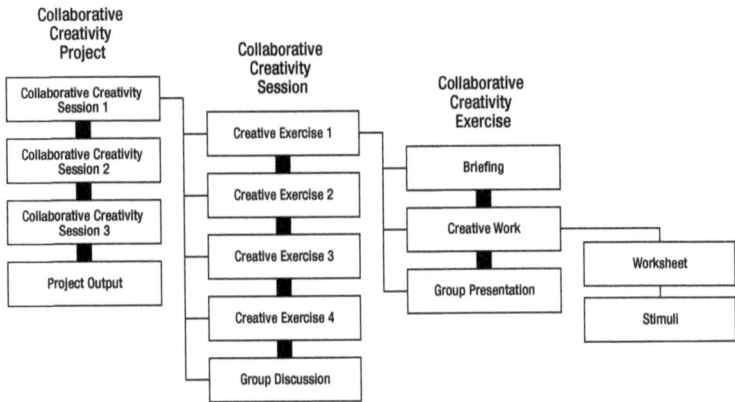

Figure 4: The structure and relationship of the three main components of Collaborative Creativity

A Collaborative Creativity project is the overarching organization of a project and it always contains at least one Collaborative Creativity session, though it can include many more; a Collaborative Creativity session is a workshop that contains a minimum of three creative exercises and culminates in a group discussion; a Collaborative Creativity exercise is a creative task that is completed with the aid of a worksheet and sometimes, although not always, stimuli of some kind.

In the following chapters, I will provide more detail about each of these and I'll also share with you:

- the principles that I always consider and incorporate when I am designing a Collaborative Creativity project and Collaborative Creativity sessions
- a procedural framework for designing projects, sessions and exercises
- basic tools and example exercises
- advice on how to put it all to practical use.

Before we begin, though, I need to define some specific terms and their meanings.

Terminology not jargon

Jargon is an old word that first appeared in Chaucer's *The Canterbury Tales* to describe the sound of birds. Since then, it has come to signify a specialized technical terminology associated with a particular activity. To the layperson, a conversation using specialized terms can seem to be senseless chatter, like that of birds, but a specialized vocabulary is useful. It allows descriptions to be concise, precise and unambiguous – provided the terms are understood in the same way by different parties.

Inevitably, I frequently use terms that are specific to Collaborative Creativity, so the following are definitions of these, together with other common words for which I want the meaning to be clear in the context of Collaborative Creativity.

- *Collaborative Creativity*: a collective imaginative activity, a problem-solving method that draws on the personal experience and knowledge of individuals who participate in a face-to-face group setting and engage in numerous specifically designed creative exercises.

- *Collaborative Creativity project (CCP)*: the sum of activities, including at least one Collaborative Creativity session, that employ Collaborative Creativity to solve a problem.

- *Collaborative Creativity session (CCS)*: a workshop, typically lasting one day, that includes various Collaborative Creativity exercises.

- *Collaborative Creativity exercise:* a task that requires imaginative thought to complete. It can be an individual activity, but more commonly it is a team or group activity. An exercise has three consecutive steps: setup, in which the task is explained; work, in which the creativity is done; and presentation, in which the worksheet is shown and explained by its creator or creators.

- *Cascading Collaborative Creativity exercise:* a task for which the stimuli derive from a previous exercise and/or the output of which becomes stimuli for a successive exercise.

- *Worksheet:* an imagination aid, specifically designed for a Collaborative Creativity exercise. Usually large posters, sometimes accompanied by other stimuli. Typically, the worksheet needs to be completed during the exercise by drawing, writing and/or collage.

- *Group discussion:* the last step of any Collaborative Creativity session, in which the coach moderates a discussion with all the participants about the work they have produced and the objective of the session.

- *Problem paper:* a document produced by the client that describes a problem they wish to resolve. The problem paper is a single-page form with just five questions.

- *Project statement:* a single phrase that clearly defines the objective of a Collaborative Creativity project. It is co-created by the client and the coach.

- *Session statement:* a single phrase that clearly defines the objective of a Collaborative Creativity session. This is a necessity in projects with multiple sessions that have different objectives; in simple projects, the session statement and the project statement are one and the same.

- *Client:* the organization and the people within that organization who commission (or sponsor) a Collaborative Creativity project.

- *Coach:* the title of a person who designs a Collaborative Creativity project and is responsible for its execution.

- *Moderator:* the title of the person/persons moderating a Collaborative Creativity session. A coach can also be a moderator.

- *Participants:* the people who are selected to actively participate in the imaginative activities of a Collaborative Creativity session.

- *Group:* all the participants of any given Collaborative Creativity session.

- *Team:* a subset of the group; a certain number of participants who work together on the exercises.

The eight principles of Collaborative Creativity

Chaos is where things are so complex you can't handle it, and order is when things are so rigid that it's too restrictive. In between that, there's a place, a place that's meaningful, where you're partly stabilized and you're partly curious. And you're operating in a manner that increases your scope of knowledge.

These are the words of Jordan Peterson, clinical psychologist and Professor of Psychology at the University of Toronto, talking on the Joe Rogan Experience podcast.[23]

Collaborative Creativity lives between chaos and order, between rational and emotional, between collective and individual. Consequently, Collaborative Creativity is not governed by rules and laws; rather, it is defined by eight principles, shown in Figure 5.

---

[23] Joe Rogan Experience podcast #877 timecode: 2:04:48, https://youtu.be/04wyGK6k6HE [accessed 2 June 2020].

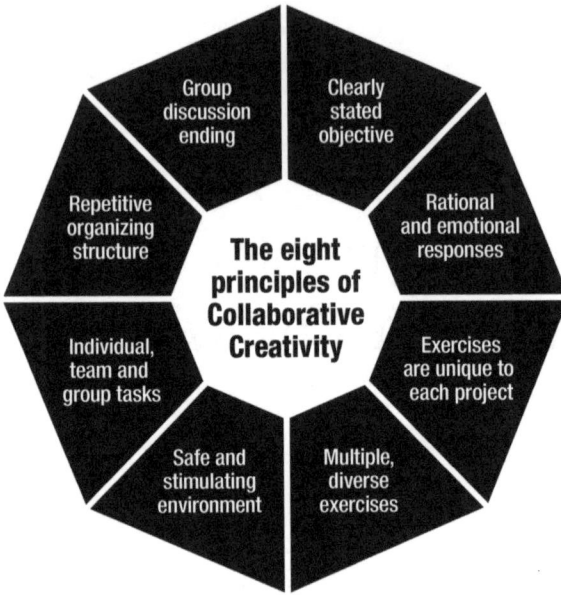

Figure 5: The eight principles of Collaborative Creativity

Each Collaborative Creativity session is highly personalized to reflect the specific objective and the characteristics of the participants. Because of this, Collaborative Creativity has a framework of principles and tools, defined by practical experience, that act as a guide while leaving plenty of space for personalization.

The more you understand these principles, the more you will find it easy to design effective Collaborative Creativity sessions.

Let's examine them, one by one, in more detail.

Clearly stated objective

Collaborative Creativity is *applied creativity*: it serves a purpose, which should be articulated clearly in a single sentence, a *project statement*. A project statement describes preferably one problem – and sometimes more than one – to be solved in order to achieve a business objective.

The definition of the objective is the first step in a Collaborative Creativity project, and is the result of a collaboration between the client and the coach. The sentence should be written in plain language because the use of jargon or complicated phrasing creates ambiguity. Even technical language, while sometimes indispensable, should be used sparingly and it is always a good idea to provide, as footnotes, definitions of any technical terms used to describe the objective. The project statement must be approved jointly by the client and coach. It is the responsibility of the client to ensure that their objective is accurately conveyed. It is the responsibility of the coach to ensure that the description has a clear meaning and provides a realistic and stimulating focus for the work.

The project statement is like a compass: unless it is accurate, those who work with it can't navigate effectively. If you are a coach, that means you risk getting lost in the project; if you are a client, the project outcome might not take you where you need to go. Like many worthwhile things, defining a project statement can take a bit of effort but an extra hour invested here avoids many wasted hours later on.

For Collaborative Creativity to be a justifiable investment, it must contribute to the achievement of a business objective and it is important for the coach to understand the business objective; however, that doesn't mean a project statement is a mere description of a business objective.

Sometimes an objective is explorative – for example, 'Discover the practical and emotional impact of being diagnosed with condition X.' At other times, it is prescriptive – for example, 'Create a tool to help newly diagnosed patients and healthcare professionals collaborate in managing condition X.'

A *session statement* is exactly like a project statement but it is specifically written for a Collaborative Creativity session. Sometimes the session statement and the project statement are the same – this is normal in situations where the project is simple and can be resolved within one or two sessions. The need to define different session statements arises in more complex projects that require various steps (with objectives that contribute to achieving the overall objective) and multiple sessions.

Like a project statement, a session statement is needed to clearly define the objective of each session and it also serves as a motivator for the participants. This is an important point: participants need to understand the objective of a Collaborative Creativity session and be engaged by it. Through the session statement, the participants must see the utility and purpose of the exercises in the session and want to achieve the objective together. Boring or entirely self-serving objectives don't motivate. This is why it is important to make the distinction between the business objective and the session statement: the business objective is what's in it for the client, while the session statement describes how this aligns with the interests of the participants.

In all forms of applied creativity, the quality of the output is affected by the quality of the input. More subtly, the perceived quality of the output is affected by the parameters within which it is judged. Consequently, it is important that you think of the project statement as both a stimulus for work and as a lens through which that work will ultimately be judged.

Rational and emotional responses

Working with others on a creative exercise is a very different experience from a discussion, and it produces different results. One reason for this is that creative thinking is a way of going beyond the surface of things; it is a way of exploring unconscious thoughts and emotions.

Take, for example, a collage that is produced simply by thinking about a subject and then choosing from among a large number of random pictures those images that resonate. The images are chosen (at least in part) by the subconscious; they are manifestations of what lies below the surface and their meaning is almost entirely subjective. The reason for the choice of a particular image must be explained by the chooser through conversation.

I have observed that the exercise of choosing is not overtly emotional, while the action of explaining and discussing the choice is visibly emotional. Another aspect of these types of exercises is that while the chooser often finds it difficult to articulate the meaning of their choice, it is evident that they badly want to explain it. It is as if once the collage has been made, the creator wants to explain it because they need to make sense of it themselves. An individual collage is one of the most emotional and revealing types of exercise (it is very useful for empathy), but for this reason it isn't appropriate for all types of sessions.

Collaborative Creativity is a business tool, and in business situations the standard mindset is formal and rational. Creativity allows participants to step outside the constraints of rational and formal, but in a business setting you must control how far you step away from the norm.

Think of creativity as being like the engine in a car. It produces power and for that power to be useful you have to control how much of it you produce. If you are going up a steep hill with a heavily loaded car, you need a lot of power to get to the top of the hill and if you are driving on ice, you need to use a minimum of power to avoid crashing off the road.

Creativity produces emotion. If you are working with experienced physicians, you need a lot of it to get them to go beyond entirely rational responses; if you are working with the parents of desperately sick children, you need only a minimum to get the same result. Self-discovery is positive and generates realization only when emotions don't overwhelm and can be processed and resolved – to achieve this, the emotion elicited by an exercise should be calibrated carefully.

The challenge of a creative exercise is unsettling and liberating. Indeed, it is unsettling *because* it is liberating. Creative exercises can legitimize and liberate thoughts and emotions so we can then explore them through conversation. The vast majority of people are much more comfortable talking about something than they are tackling a creative assignment because, among other things, they feel more in control. This is one reason why creative exercises and discussion are alternated and a session always ends with a group discussion. It is important to challenge people to reveal things, but it is equally important to give them the space to elaborate how they feel.

In some sessions, the aim isn't to help emotions and unconscious thought emerge; rather, it is to help a group understand the emotions and mindset of others. Here, creativity is a useful aid for comprehending others and the aim is to transfer emotions. Working on creative exercises is a very different experience from a discussion, and provides different results. We can maintain emotional distance from a subject when we talk about it, while it is harder to maintain that distance while creating something regarding that subject.

Some sessions are very pragmatic and focused on invention. Often, in these types of sessions, the participants are all colleagues. Here it is important to manage the experience of a Collaborative Creativity session as if it were a collective thought process, using different exercises to examine different aspects of an issue and arrive at a consensus, then at the end combine these decisions into a coherent idea shared by the collective. The emotions present need to be channelled into the ideas, and creativity becomes a way of making decisions together that include emotions but thoughtfully manage how those emotions are dealt with.

In summary, the aim of Collaborative Creativity is to make it possible to talk about relevant emotions, beliefs and experience. The way creative exercises are designed determines how deep below the surface the participants will reach. Too little emotion is uninspiring and therefore ineffective; too much emotion is disruptive and therefore unproductive. The ideal is to maintain equilibrium.

Exercises are unique to each project

Every objective poses different problems, and diverse groups of participants need to be stimulated in different ways. These issues, together with dozens of other variables, mean that each Collaborative Creativity session and the exercises within it must be specifically designed to be as effective as possible at realizing the objective and unleashing the potential of the participants.

A Collaborative Creativity session is the sum of the exercises it contains, and these must be designed individually while also being part of a series where each exercise takes into account its relationship with the exercises following or preceding it. As a whole, you should design the exercises of a Collaborative Creativity session to solicit a frame of mind conducive to resolving the objective.

If every session statement is unique and the characteristics of the participants are unique, then the creative exercises of a Collaborative Creativity session cannot be standard. There are basic formats of exercises that can be personalized and used in many circumstances (I have described some of my favourite basic formats in the Collaborative Creativity Exercise formats chapter), but they must always be adapted to fit each specific purpose.

The only time it is advisable to repeat the use of an exercise, or a series of exercises, is within the same project, which has multiple Collaborative Creativity sessions – here it can be useful to repeat an exercise with a different group of participants to see how the results differ. We saw this earlier in 'The PKU & ME Study'. In that example, two of the exercises were identical; however, two exercises were different for two reasons: first, one exercise was relevant only to compliant attitudes and actions, so it was pointless to repeat it with non-compliant subjects; and second, the output from the compliant session provided insights that suggested a new avenue of exploration for the non-compliant group.

Exercise design determines the type of output; the look and feel of the exercise influences the quality of the engagement. In my experience, it is important to show that effort and care has been put into preparing the session because people will naturally respond to this with a similar level of commitment and attention.

Try giving the project a name, create a logo and brand all the materials (name tags, worksheets, etc.). If the participants are part of an organization – a patient advocacy group or a pharmaceutical company – incorporate their logo in the materials so it looks tailored to them. Likewise, use imagery, metaphors and stories that are relevant to the participants. Because Collaborative Creativity involves people who have some form of interest in the outcome, the design of the worksheets and the presentation of the exercises should remind the participants that the work is about them and the session format is designed for them.

Designing interesting, personalized worksheets also minimizes the blank-piece-of-paper-syndrome. By providing a bespoke worksheet that already has some relevant elements or structure on it, you can provide a framework for the solution that makes thinking and expressing the thought easier. Hastily scrawled words, simple sketches and diagrams, or collages of photographs and post-it notes look very different if they are on an otherwise blank piece of paper or on a specifically designed worksheet that frames them. It also reduces presentation anxiety because when every worksheet has a basic format, it makes the difference between the prettiest and the scruffiest elaboration less stark than when using blank paper.

Exercises can be designed to be self-contained or they can be designed to be linked to other exercises. Self-contained exercises are tasks where all the stimuli are defined prior to the Collaborative Creativity session and the output of one exercise is not intended to be used in other exercises. Exercises that link to other exercises are called cascading exercises. In these, the output or part of the output of one exercise is designed to be the stimulus for a successive exercise.

Another thing to consider about exercise design is that while each exercise and the combination of the exercises must be focused on a specific objective, it is vital to not lose sight of the fact that each task must be stimulating and enjoyable for the participants. There is no point in designing an exercise that is theoretically perfect but in practice uninspiring or unrewarding. Realization may not be your objective, but it is useful for keeping participants involved in the work. The ability and the motivation of the participants can vary enormously, which is another reason why exercise design is unique: the difficulty and the style of the challenges need to be calibrated accordingly.

One final consideration concerns the exercise presentations and the group discussion at the end of the session. As a whole, the exercises of a Collaborative Creativity session must be designed to solicit a frame of mind that makes all these group discussions rich, honest and enlightening. You should always try to design exercises that result in things people want to present and talk about.

Whether it's a new service or a personal experience, the face value of completed worksheets is always inferior to the value of the discussion about what they represent. The role of creative exercises and their worksheets is to serve as a tool while creating, and as a memory aid when the work is presented and discussed.

Ultimately, personalized exercise design that correctly considers all the variables and creates a great experience for the participants simply produces superior results.

Multiple, diverse exercises

Creative energy lasts 20 to 40 minutes and then fades. It's not just a question of concentration; it's also a question of stimulation – when we are given a new intellectual task, we are intrigued by the possibilities and spontaneously all sorts of ideas start to emerge. To make the most of the maximum burst of energy, the ideal time for each Collaborative Creativity exercise is between half an hour and an hour.

In a typical, full-day session, this allows us to work through multiple exercises, which is advantageous for various reasons:

- We can approach any given problem in many different ways, allowing us to make sure that diverse aspects of the problem are covered by creative activity.

- We can approach a problem using a step-wise approach, with each exercise laying down the foundation for the next.

- We can help participants to solve a seemingly overwhelming problem by dividing it into parts so they can concentrate on solving exercises with smaller scope than the main problem while each exercise takes them a step closer to solving the problem.

- We can uncover complexity in a seemingly banal problem by exploring it from different points of view.

- We can ask the same question many times in different ways and discover the commonalities and discrepancies in the solutions.

- We can have a mix of individual, team and group exercises within a single session.

- We can provide different kinds of mental stimulation with each exercise and obtain many ideas with a range of origins.

- We can devise exercises with different levels of freedom and constraints to see how the ideas compare.

A Collaborative Creativity session is a sequence of exercises that stimulate and influence the state of mind of the participants. There are other factors in play, such as the dynamics created by the different personalities in the room and the influence of the moderators; however, the sequence of exercises plays a hugely significant role in the results of the session. You should consider this when designing multiple exercises and not only regarding cascading exercises. Even if the results of an exercise are not used as input for the next exercise, the thinking and the stimuli of that exercise will influence the rest of the session. For this reason, it is preferable to design a session with an individual exercise at the beginning rather than the end because at the start of a session the diversity of each individual experience will emerge, whereas at the end it will inevitably be influenced by the collective thinking that preceded it.

When you design a session, you need to be mindful of the collective thought process you are creating and how it can help a group approach a problem and achieve consensus on its resolution. However, a thought process is not thoughts; it defines the order of events and the stimuli involved and, while these do influence the outcome, ultimately the ideas that emerge must always be those freely expressed by the participants.

Safe and stimulating environment

Treating people with care and respect is always the right thing to do, and if you want maximum cognitive ability it is also the smart thing to do. People who are unhappy, uncomfortable, tired or experiencing any other kind of distress do not perform well. A study conducted at the University of Bergen, Norway on the effects of positive and negative mood on divergent thinking concluded that, 'Results showed natural positive mood to facilitate significantly task performance and negative mood to inhibit it.'[24]

Other studies have found that 'positive mood participants were able to see relations between concepts', as well as demonstrating advanced abilities 'in distinguishing the differences between concepts'.[25]

Participating in a Collaborative Creativity session is challenging, and its environment helps determine whether the challenge is rewarding and the experience is positive for the participants.

The session environment is influenced by many factors that, as far as possible, should be managed thoughtfully:

- Physical space. Where we are affects how we are, a session should take place in an appropriate (and distraction free) environment.

- Mood. The mood of the group is influenced by the presence or absence of pre-existing relationships, the ability of the

[24] S. K. Vosburg, 'The effects of positive and negative mood on divergent-thinking performance', Creativity Research Journal, 11 (2) (1998), 165–172.

[25] N. Murray, H. Sujan, E. R. Hirt and M. Sujan, 'The influence of mood on categorization: A cognitive flexibility interpretation', Journal of Personality and Social Psychology, 59 (3) (1990), 411–425.

moderator to manage the group and the level of interest the participants have in the session's objective.

- *Expectations.* The session begins before it actually starts. How you invite people, how you treat them, the instructions and information you give them in advance are the first elements of the environment of the session.

- *Session rules.* These can vary depending on the type of session and the participants, but some rules are always valid (see below) and these set a certain tone.

- *Feedback.* How work is received influences the work that follows it. Keeping the environment open, calm and constructive while discussing the creative output is vital to maintaining a healthy creative vibe.

The following are the rules I always apply in my sessions to establish boundaries and define the environment. I always start with the session statement. The people in the room should already know why they are there, but I find that starting with something they know is reassuring and is also the first thing for the group to agree upon – it is the uniting purpose. Then, in the introduction, I always explain the rules so they are clear to everyone:

- With the exception of handwritten notes, no recording will be made by the moderators and no participant must make any recording. A recording can easily be disseminated publicly and phrases can be extrapolated and used out of context – the potential threat of this limits candid exchanges.

- All electronic devices are to be switched off and stowed away during the exercises. This is motivated by the need to guarantee privacy as in the previous rule and also to eliminate the constant distractions created by these devices.

- The Chatham House Rule applies. The official wording of the rule is as follows: 'When a meeting, or part thereof, is held under the Chatham House Rule, participants are free to use the information received, but neither the identity nor the affiliation of the speaker(s), nor that of any other participant, may be revealed.'[26]

---

[26] See www.chathamhouse.org/chatham-house-rule [accessed 2 June 2020].

- Be positive. Don't criticize and don't interrupt.

- Be punctual. This is a form of respect to others – don't keep everyone waiting for you.

- If at some point you don't know what you are supposed to be doing, it's not your fault, the moderator evidently hasn't explained the exercise clearly.

These rules are designed to allow people to express themselves freely. A creative session where participants are guarded in their words and careful about how they express themselves is basically doomed. Especially when exploring emotions and beliefs, it is the purity of the sentiment not the perfection of its expression that matters.

Establishing a safe place is crucial for a Collaborative Creativity session to produce great ideas, but there is one more thing that affects the environment: wakefulness. Cognitive function is negatively affected by lack of sleep. One study found that performance, tested by a word fluency task and a non-verbal planning test, was 'significantly impaired by sleep loss'.[27]

Obviously, it is the responsibility of each individual to arrive properly rested for a day of work but where they can, organizers should facilitate this. For example, having participants travel the day before and sleep in the same hotel that will host the session is preferable to having people wake early and arrive the same day. This does impact the overall cost of the session, but unless every effort is made to ensure participants are happy and rested, the entire investment in a Collaborative Creativity session could be wasted.

In summary, each Collaborative Creativity session must create a safe and stimulating environment for participants. The setting must be relaxed, and conducive to wellbeing and concentration. The atmosphere should be informal, respectful and non-judgemental, and the opinions and ideas must be guaranteed anonymity.

---

[27] J. A. Horne, 'Sleep loss and "divergent thinking" ability', *Sleep*, 11 (6) (1988), 528–536.

Individual, team and group tasks

Collaborative Creativity uses different configurations of participants for different exercises. Certain exercises are performed individually, some in teams and others as a group that includes all the participants.

The choice of which exercises are performed by individuals, teams or the group is made by the coach when designing a session. There are various reasons to choose one or the other:

- *Productivity.* Twelve people will produce more ideas if they are divided into four teams, with three people in each team, than if they work as a single group.

- *Diversity of ideas.* In a single group, one strong personality can dominate a whole exercise, while if divided into four teams that influence will be limited to the response of one team and consequently more voices will be heard.

- *Diversity of perspectives.* When a group contains people with different experiences and competencies, the possibility of mixing them in small teams favours results that combine diversity while uniting sub-groups in homogeneous teams favours results that highlight the diversity of mindsets.

- *Individuality.* Personal thought and experience are best expressed by individual exercises.

- *Consensus.* This is reached more easily through group exercises.

- *Safe environment.* Individual and group exercises can be more stressful for some people, so a small team is a more manageable and enjoyable environment. For this reason, the composition of teams usually remains the same for the duration of a session.

It is important to remember that the group is the central element of the session. Exercises that are performed individually or in teams begin with a group briefing and end with a group presentation where everyone shares their ideas with everyone else. This allows the group to be influenced – even inspired – by the thoughts of others. It allows the group to easily and naturally identify common themes or gaps.

Designing a session that switches continuously between team activities, individual activities and moderated group discussion reduces the possibility of an individual dominating a discussion or manipulating the outcome.

The dynamic of alternating moments in the group and others in teams also helps strengthen the idea that ideas are cumulative – that the next wave of thoughts is influenced by those that preceded it. When the objective is to produce innovative ideas, I encourage teams to be influenced by each other, to build on the ideas of others and to combine different ideas. Often innovation is the result of an unexpected combination and, furthermore, the borrowing and influencing helps to cement a sense of co-authorship of the solutions that emerge from the session.

Repetitive organizing structure

In a Collaborative Creativity session, as much time as possible should be dedicated to working – which means the time devoted to tasks like explaining exercises and what to do next should be minimized. The more the design of the session repeats certain actions, the more fluid and rapid the session will be, and the less time needs to be dedicated to non-productive activities. Another advantage of repeating actions is that routine is reassuring: small rituals that are understood by the group contribute to a relaxed atmosphere.

To achieve this, the way a Collaborative Creativity session is organized should be as simple as possible, and needs to be easily understood by the participants.

The agenda for the entire Collaborative Creativity session, complete with start and end times of each activity, should be presented and explained at the start of the session. Sometimes it is necessary to adapt the agenda and/or the timing as the session progresses, which is fine, but when possible it is best to adhere to the agenda. This reassures the participants that the session is well planned and working.

It also allows them to do their own planning – the agenda must include moments of free time like coffee breaks and lunch. When an exercise is in progress, we expect concentration but we must respect each individual's need to check email and return calls.

The agenda provides a defined structure to the session, and each exercise in a session should follow a routine as much as possible. The routine I use usually has three steps:

1   Explanation to the group of the exercise, distribution of the relevant materials and indication of the allotted time.

2   Creativity – all participants work on the assigned task and prepare their exercise worksheets.

3   Presentation – all worksheets are presented to the assembled group and briefly discussed.

When time is your enemy, ritual is your friend. The first and last steps are both in a group setting, so it is easy and natural to move from the presentation of one exercise to the explanation of the next. This repetitive sequence is simple, easy to manage and optimizes time (once the participants have done it once or twice, they follow it naturally).

Group discussion ending

The final group discussion is a very important moment in a session – often the most important. The length of discussion varies, depending on the objective of the session and therefore what the discussion needs to accomplish. In any case, the group discussion is the culmination of all the work: after hours of creative exercises, the collective and individual focus and awareness of the issue at hand is at its peak. A lot of energy has been spent and a certain camaraderie has been created in the teams and the group – the conversation is more relaxed and open. It isn't the first group conversation: each exercise preceding the final group discussion has concluded with a conversation about the work. This, however, is the first moment when the group is free to talk in general terms about the objective. In many ways, it is the culmination of all the work done previously. Frequently, this is the moment when breakthroughs will occur.

What happens in the group discussion is always different, but like the rest of the session the group discussion should have a structure:

- The first thing to do is address any off-exercise items that have cropped up during the session. Off-exercise items are thoughts or issues, raised by one or more participants, that are alien to the core objective and have been 'parked' by the moderator (a bullet point scribbled on a flip-chart) so that they didn't derail an exercise.

- The second thing to do is 'walk the room'. As the worksheets have been completed, they will have been hung on the walls of the room. The physical transformation of the walls by the worksheets always gives a sense of achievement to the participants (and relief to the coach/moderator). The primary objective of walking the room, though, is to review the work together. Inquire about incongruences in different exercises or from different teams and understand these better. Highlight similarities, themes and promising connections, and get the group's reactions to these.

- The third thing to do is to ask the group whether there are any important and potentially inconvenient truths or issues which members may be aware of but they haven't yet discussed. More often than not, the discussion that follows is rich and extremely useful and I am convinced that the things revealed at this point would not have been mentioned with the same line of questioning at the start of the session.

- The last thing to do is provide a sense of closure and realization for the participants. Sometimes this might require the moderator to offer a sort of summary of the outcome to the group – I find it useful to return to the session statement and connect the work produced with the objective of the session. This achieves two things: it gives the group a sense of achievement; and it allows the moderator to offer to the group an interpretation of the key points that have emerged and receive the group's agreement or dissent regarding that interpretation.

If a Collaborative Creativity session is focused on qualitative research, it is important to reassure the participants that they have effectively transferred their experience and needs and that this will serve to inform and improve something. If the session is focused on new ideas, then a vote can be used both to gain a sense of the consensus in the room and switch the mindset from creator to critic/judge. If the session is focused on convergence and alignment, then the last exercise should produce a summary of the agreed items and the discussion can concentrate on next steps and the future. No matter what the session's objective and outcome, the moderator's closing remarks must convey gratitude for the participants' efforts, thinking, sharing and creativity, and provide them with a sense of pride in all the work they've done and the things they've created.

The Collaborative Creativity project

A Collaborative Creativity project solves a problem using Collaborative Creativity in one or more sessions, with one or more groups of people. Figure 6 shows the procedural framework of a Collaborative Creativity project.

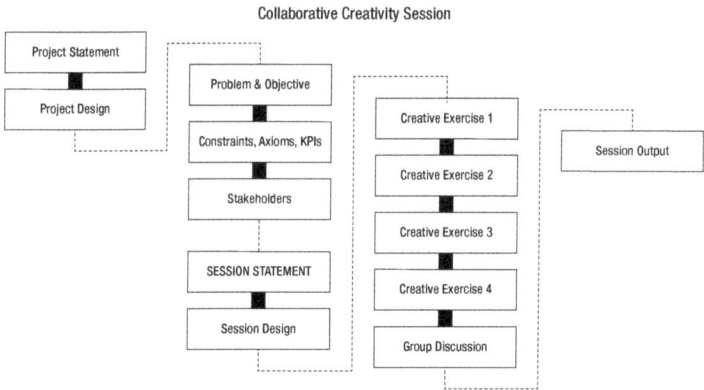

Figure 6: Procedural framework of a Collaborative Creativity project

It all starts with a problem and the desire or need to solve it. Clients often express their problems as desired outcomes. I recommend always backing up a bit and looking at the problem that the desired outcome is intended to solve. For this reason, the first formal step I ask a client to take is to produce a 'problem paper'. You can download the template from https://peter-comber.net/collaborativecreativity.

Problem paper

The problem paper is a single-page form with seven parts. The first two simply identify the company and the brand, while the other five ask:

- What is the problem the company/brand faces?
- What is the desired outcome of resolving the problem for the company/brand?
- Why is that outcome important?
- Who is actively involved and which other stakeholders should be considered?
- What barriers currently prevent you from achieving the desired outcome?

The answers to these five questions constitute the vital, basic information about the project.

It is a simple form and the brief mental exercise required to compile it always helps to clarify the situation. On occasion, compiling a problem statement may reveal that what seemed to be one problem is actually two separate, albeit related, issues. In these cases, it is best to produce two problem papers so that the issues can be tackled concurrently but correctly understood separately.

Project briefing

Once the client has produced the problem paper, they give it to the coach to analyse. Because the problem paper is a single page, it is concise and it contains the information the client considers most important. As it lacks detail, you as the coach will spontaneously raise questions as you read, so write down all the pertinent questions you can think of – you will need them for the next step. The project briefing is a meeting where the client and the coach discuss the problem paper and exchange more information about the project. In this meeting, all the questions that arose previously should be answered or highlighted as questions that must be answered by the project process.

Mapping

Armed with a comprehensive set of information, the coach must now make sense of it all. I call this 'information mapping' (often abbreviated to just 'mapping') and I find it helps me to comprehend all the acquired knowledge if I divide it into five groups: problem and objective; constraints; axioms; key performance indicators (KPIs); and stakeholders.

- The *problem and objective* group is self-explanatory and absolutely vital – these are the key drivers of the project.

- The *constraints* are all those things that are pertinent to the project; these are, for the intents of the project, immutable. They include such things as timing and budget, as well as business objective, project milestones, corporate regulations, existing strategies and tactics and areas of activity that are off limits.

- The *axioms* are all those things that the client and coach have agreed, for the context of the project, to be facts or reasonable assumptions. These may include things like future market conditions, the current actions of certain stakeholders, the actions of competitors and the evolution of the market, the attitude of the healthcare profession and so on.

- The *KPIs* are those parameters the client has chosen to measure the success of the project. They depend entirely on the type of project and the overall objectives of the client.

- The *stakeholders* are the different categories of people who are in some way involved in the project. These should be identified according to their role (in terms of their involvement in the project) and organized into groups. Typical groups are specific types of healthcare professionals, patients, caregivers and internal functions (colleagues of the client with specific responsibilities).

Once all this information has been mapped, it should be clear not only what you know but also whether there is anything you don't yet know but need to know. Maybe the list of questions you had for the client contained something the client couldn't answer or you only noticed an important gap when you finished mapping. Either way, if the information is vital to the project, you need to resolve the gap in one of the following ways:

- Ask the client whether they have the information or can obtain it.

- Research existing third-party sources to try to obtain the information.

- Determine with the client a reasonable assumption (which joins the other axioms).

- Consider the acquisition of the missing information as part of the project mission.

Project statement and project design

Now you have all the information mapped out, you can start designing the project. If the project and/or the accompanying information are particularly complex, it is best to share the information map with the client to make sure it is aligned with the client's knowledge and expectations before proceeding. If the project is simple, it is usually more convenient to proceed directly with the design.

The first task is to write a project statement, a single phrase describing the objective of the Collaborative Creativity project. This should be as short and unambiguous as possible. If you are in doubt about how to articulate it, you can write more than one project statement because the final wording of the statement will be co-created with the client, so it is fine to have more than one proposal as a starting point.

The most important thing to do is figure out how many Collaborative Creativity sessions will be needed to complete the project, what each session will achieve and in what order they should occur. The number of sessions is dictated by:

- the different steps required to complete the project
- the things you don't know and/or the things you need to achieve
- the time required for each of these things
- the participants (what types of participants, how many, whether different types of participant can or should be mixed or kept separate).

I think the simplest way to explain this is with two examples; for brevity, I have kept the information in both of them to a minimum.

Project A

- *Project statement:* Understand the needs and frustrations of neurologists in managing acute strokes to be able to improve support of their practice and improve patient outcomes.

- *Constraints:* Participants must represent diverse geographical regions and varying levels of experience.

- *Axioms:* Nurses and other types of HCP need not be involved because these are influenced directly by the neurologists who drive protocols and adoption of innovations.

- *KPIs:* Insights on issues that prevent timely intervention to prevent recurrent stroke in the high-risk period immediately after the initial stroke.

- *Stakeholders:* Neurologists, client medical liaison.

This is a simple project. The scope is only for market research involving one type of subject (neurologists). Potentially, this could be resolved with a single Collaborative Creativity session. In this case, though, the constraint suggests otherwise: to satisfy the requirements of subject diversity, we will need to involve approximately 50 neurologists. These could be involved in a single session but two sessions with 25 neurologists each, in two different locations (for example one in the north and the other in the south), is more manageable and logistically efficient in terms of time and overall cost. In this case, we would decide on two Collaborative Creativity sessions solely for logistical reasons, with the session design the same for both sessions.

Project B

- *Project statement:* Design and deliver a patient support programme to help patients who undergo liver transplants correctly manage their treatment and post-op lifestyle, and help their healthcare practitioners to monitor their condition.

- *Constraints:* The programme must be activated for the patient by the healthcare practitioner, and the information the healthcare practitioner can monitor must be clinically relevant.

- *Axioms:* The liver transplant patients that will be served by the service are self-motivated and the programme will focus on practical help and information. Hospital nurses spend more time with post-op patients than hepatologists.

- *KPIs:* Number of clinics enrolled; number of patients enrolled; other metrics to be defined once programme is designed.

- *Stakeholders:* Hepatologists, nutritionists, nurses, patients, caregivers, patient association, homecare provider.

This is a far more complex project. Our information map tells us that: we have information gaps regarding the post-op patient experience and needs; we believe we know which information can help the healthcare practitioners to monitor the patient, but we don't know the best way to get the information to the healthcare practitioners, we know nurses have a key role but we aren't sure of the best way to involve them.

Obviously there are many other things we don't know, but these are the three vital knowledge gaps in the project that influence its design.

It is evident that we must plan a Collaborative Creativity session with post-op patients to learn about their experience and needs in order to create a programme they will find useful. We also need to understand how the programme can fit into the clinical practice of the healthcare practitioners who follow the patient so we must plan another Collaborative Creativity session with hepatologists, nutritionists and nurses. This session would benefit from the insights gathered from the patients in the previous session.

With the results of these two sessions, we can then run a third session, with participants from the patient association, the homecare provider (who will materially execute the support programme) and the client, to transfer the insights to them and co-create the details of the programme.

I find it useful to lay out the key information of a project on a single worksheet. Figure 7 shows an example of a worksheet that describes Project B. You can download the empty template here https://peter-comber.net/collaborativecreativity.

Project Statement: Design and deliver a patient support programme to help patients who undergo liver transplants correctly manage their treatment, post-op lifestyle and help their HCPs to monitor their condition.

Problem:	Objective:
Liver transplant patients often have difficulty adapting to post-op treatments and lifestyle.	Provide patients and the team of HCPs who care for them with tools to better manage life post-op.

Constraints:	Axioms:	KPIs:
The programme must be activated for the patient by the HCP and the information the HCP can monitor must be clinically relevant.	Patients are self-motivated – the programme will focus on practical help and information. Hospital nurses spend more time with post-op patients than hepatologists.	Number of clinics enrolled. Number of patients enrolled. **Other metrics to be defined once** programme is designed.

Stakeholders:	Session:	Session:	Session:	Session:
Hepatologists Nutritionists Nurses Patients Caregivers Patient ass.tn Homecare provider	Explore post-op patient experience and needs	Explore HCP team **workflow and their** ideas, desires and expectations for the support programme	Transfer patient and HCP insights. Define the services the programme will provide, content and structure.	
	Participants: Patients Caregivers?	Participants: Hepatologists Nutritionists Nurses	Participants: Patient association Homecare provider Client	Participants:

Figure 7: Example of a worksheet that describes Project B

As you can see, the project worksheet contains only the essential information and for this reason it is useful – mistakes can hide in complexity, so a simplified snapshot of a project makes it easier to review and share with others.

Now that you have a project design with a project statement, the next step is to share it with the client and refine both together. Following this, you will design the Collaborative Creativity sessions (explained in the next chapter) and then execute the project.

Project output

The final result of a project depends on the objective. It can be a collection of ideas, a research document, an app, a business unit, a strategy, a consensus document, a new service, an international communication concept, a different way of working together and much more.

Let's look at our two examples again and see their outputs.

For Project A, the output is a research document that contains the combined results of the two identical Collaborative Creativity sessions. In this case, the project output and the session output are one and the same.

For Project B, there are various outputs. The first are milestone outputs – these are the documents that contain the results of each of the three Collaborative Creativity sessions. Then there is the final output document that contains an abstract of the three milestone documents and the description of the final design of the patient support programme. In this case, there will also be a follow-up document after an agreed timeframe that evaluates the KPIs of the patient support programme.

The Collaborative Creativity session

A Collaborative Creativity session is a component of a Collaborative Creativity project. It solves a problem using Collaborative Creativity exercises performed by a group of participants.

Figure 8 shows the procedural framework of a Collaborative Creativity session.

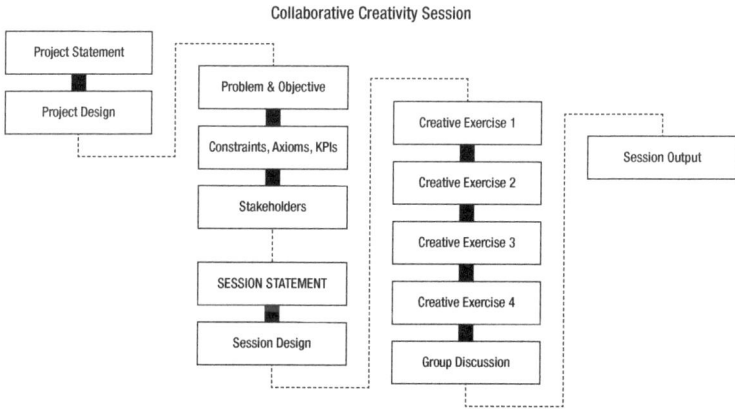

Figure 8: Procedural framework of a Collaborative Creativity session

Before we look at how to design a Collaborative Creativity session, let's look at the structure of a session, how it flows and, first of all, who does what.

The main actors in a Collaborative Creativity session are:

- the coach
- the moderator
- the participants.

Coach

The Coach is responsible for the design of the session, the exercises in the session and the production of a document that organizes, analyses and summarizes the session output.

Moderator

A moderator is responsible for running the session (this role is described in a dedicated chapter later in the book). A moderator is also responsible for taking written notes, during the session, to record important ideas, statements and decisions. In many types of sessions one, maybe two moderators are sufficient. Sessions with a large number of participants require more moderators (as a rule of thumb, at least one moderator for every twenty participants). In sessions where the focus is market research, three moderators (for triangulation of notes to ensure data integrity and validity) are recommended and at a minimum two are required to faithfully record the session.

Participants

This is the group of people who perform the exercises in the Collaborative Creativity session. The characteristics of participants are defined by the scope of the session – the participants are people who have a specific experience or competence that is considered indispensable and/or relevant, by the coach and client, for reaching the session's objective.

Other actors

Many other roles can be necessary to correctly execute a Collaborative Creativity session. A medical copywriter may be needed to research and write content for the session. A graphic designer is needed to produce worksheets and any other materials that need to be designed. Recruiters are sometimes required to source and engage participants. Event organizers are responsible for the logistics of a session: they find a suitable location, arrange for catering, organize travel and, when appropriate, accommodation for the participants.

As you will have realized by now, the structure of a Collaborative Creativity session can vary greatly to accommodate different objectives. However, as an example, let's look at the agenda of a typical one-day session.

Collaborative Creativity session agenda

- Welcome introduction
- Exercise briefing
- Creative work
- Worksheet presentation and discussion
- *Coffee break*
- Exercise briefing
- Creative work
- Worksheet presentation and discussion
- *Lunch break*
- Exercise briefing
- Creative work
- Worksheet presentation and discussion
- *Coffee break*
- Exercise briefing
- Creative work
- Worksheet presentation and discussion
- Group discussion
- Closing remarks.

Welcome introduction and closing remarks
A session starts with the moderator welcoming the participants, explaining the objective of the day and the rules. (This was covered

in the section 'Safe and stimulating environment' in the chapter titled 'The eight principles of Collaborative Creativity'.)

The closing remarks are a thoughtful way of ending the session and serve to provide a sense of closure and realization for the participants. Often this takes the form of a brief summary of the work produced and the outcome of the session.

Exercise briefing
Each creative exercise starts with a briefing, during which the moderator explains the exercise to the participants and introduces all the tools available for it.

Creative work
This is the time given to the participants to perform the given creative task.

Worksheet presentation and discussion
The last part of each exercise is dedicated to sharing the work that has been produced among the group and commenting on it. All the worksheets finalized during the creative work are hung on the wall of the room where the session takes place.

Group discussion
This is always the last activity of a session. The whole group of participants unites to discuss the work produced and the objective of the session. More information on this is available in the section dedicated to group discussion in the chapter titled 'The eight principles of Collaborative Creativity'.

Designing a Collaborative Creativity session

The problem that a Collaborative Creativity session must solve and the overall objective of the session is defined in the Collaborative Creativity project of which it is a part.

The first task for any session is to establish the constraints, axioms, KPIs and stakeholders that are pertinent to that Collaborative Creativity session. Some, or all, of these derive directly from the information of the overall project, while others may be specific only to that session. An example of a constraint specific to a session might be a particular date and location for the session – if you aim to involve international scientific opinion leaders, it is often a good idea to organize a session in the same city and on a date in close proximity to an international medical congress that you know they will attend.

Once you have all the information and it is mapped out, you can start to design the session. This process is similar to project design.

The first task is to write a session statement. Again, this is a single phrase that describes the objective of the Collaborative Creativity session. It should be as short and unambiguous as possible, and it should be written in a way that makes it relevant to the session participants.

The session statement is a re-elaboration of the session description from the project sheet. In the Project B example, the description of the first session was: 'Understand post-op patient experience and needs.'

If we write this in a way that provides the context and makes it relevant to the session participants, we get something like this: 'Learn about everyday post-op issues and needs of people who have undergone a liver transplant and imagine ways to help them correctly manage their treatment and lifestyle.'

This session statement succinctly and accurately describes the objective of the session and includes a purpose of social utility: it can be used in recruiting and later in the session to engage and focus the participants. Note that it contains a description of the participants; whenever possible, this is a good idea because it affirms that they are central to the session and therefore the absolute experts on the subject it will explore.

The next task is to analyse the session problem and objective in relation to the participants. Start writing down questions you need the participants to answer to solve the problem (remember the unresolved questions from the project briefing and project analysis, as this might be relevant here). Once you have a list, leave it for a day and then check that you've covered all the important things; maybe go over it all again with someone else – preferably your client – and look for gaps.

When you are confident that the list is complete, sort the questions into two groups of what I call narrow and broad questions. Narrow questions have a limited range of possible responses and broad questions have an extensive range and often have emotional/preconscious aspects.

At this point, you need to establish the duration of the session you are designing because this influences the number of exercises for which you will have time. Consider any constraints you may have – for example, time-limitations of participants or other organizational limits.

Let's say you have a typical eight hours. Consider all the activities of the day and allocate appropriate time for them. This will vary depending on the participants and other considerations, but the following is an example of time allocation:

- 10-minute welcome introduction
- 30 minutes for two 15-minute coffee breaks
- one-hour lunch
- one-hour final group discussion
- 20 minute cushion (always keep a little extra time for flexibility).

The total of the above is three hours, which leaves five hours for creative exercises.

Now you need to go back to your list of broad questions and mediate between:

- the overall objective of the session and project
- the time allocated to exercises in the session
- the importance of the grouped questions
- the emotional/preconscious importance of the questions.

This is exercise design and the next chapter is dedicated to it, so I won't go into detail here. In summary, the objective is to design exercises that can solicit indirect responses to the questions we need to answer.

Let's go back to Project B and use one of its sessions as an example. Figure 9 shows an example session worksheet. You can download the empty template at https://peter-comber.net/collaborativecreativity.

Session Statement:
Learn about everyday post-op issues and needs of people who have undergone a liver transplant and imagine ways to help them correctly manage their treatment and lifestyle.

Constraints, Axioms, KPIs:
KPIs: indications of practical issues/needs and emotions/attitudes towards condition.

Date: Before end of June	Location: To be defined

Participants: Patients (12) Caregivers (4)				
4 teams: 3 teams with 4 patients 1 team with 4 caregivers	**Question:** NEEDS — What 3 things would you change regarding your condition?	**Question:** EMOTIONS — How does post-transplant health management make you feel? What's good + what's bad?	**Question:** PRACTICAL HELP — What services could help you manage your condition?	**Question:** HOPES — How do you see yourself and your condition in the future?
	Single □ Team ☒ Group □	Single ☒ Team □ Group □	Single □ Team ☒ Group □	Single □ Team ☒ Group □
	T-Prep: 10 T-Work: 40 T-Pres: 20	T-Prep: 5 T-Work: 20 T-Pres: 45	T-Prep: 5 T-Work: 50 T-Pres: 30	T-Prep: 5 T-Work: 40 T-Pres: 30
	Exercise: Transforma	**Exercise:** Collage "Ups&Downs"	**Exercise:** Lifebelt	**Exercise:** Time travel
	Materials: Transforma A3 worksheets Blue marker pens	**Materials:** Black/white A3 worksheets Scissors + tape	**Materials:** Prototype A2 worksheet Blue marker pens + tape	**Materials:** Facebook page worksheet Blue marker pens + tape
	Stimuli: ——	**Stimuli:** Colour photo magazines	**Stimuli:** Service option paper strips	**Stimuli:** ——
	Empathy ☆☆☆ ☆☆☆ Realization ☆☆☆ ☆☆☆ Invention ☆☆☆ ☆☆☆ Cohesion ☆☆☆ ☆☆☆ Self-discovery ☆☆☆ ☆☆☆	Empathy ☆☆☆ ☆☆☆ Realization ☆☆☆ ☆☆☆ Invention ☆☆☆ ☆☆☆ Cohesion ☆☆☆ ☆☆☆ Self-discovery ☆☆☆ ☆☆☆	Empathy ☆☆☆ ☆☆☆ Realization ☆☆☆ ☆☆☆ Invention ☆☆☆ ☆☆☆ Cohesion ☆☆☆ ☆☆☆ Self-discovery ☆☆☆ ☆☆☆	Empathy ☆☆☆ ☆☆☆ Realization ☆☆☆ ☆☆☆ Invention ☆☆☆ ☆☆☆ Cohesion ☆☆☆ ☆☆☆ Self-discovery ☆☆☆ ☆☆☆

Figure 9: Example session worksheet (Project B)

As with the project worksheet, the session worksheet contains only the essential information, which makes it useful as a planning tool and also helpful for sharing a design with others.

You can see at a glance that this session has four exercises and that the list of broad questions has been summarized by four even broader questions. The coach who designed this has decided that these are the most important for the project and also the most likely to provide valuable information.

These exercises will spontaneously provide answers to many of our questions, but not all. You must organize the list of all the questions the session needs to resolve (narrow and broad) and give the list to the moderator of the session. Over the course of the session, the moderator will cross off the list those that are spontaneously answered and, at appropriate times (especially during the presentation and discussion of exercises), ask questions from the list that are pertinent to the context. The unanswered questions that remain after the last exercise will become the guide for the final group discussion.

Refining the session

Now that you have ideas for the session design and session statement, the next step is to share them with the client and refine everything together. Once you have reached an agreement on this, you can proceed to prepare, run and finalize the output of the session. The following is a summary of the things to do:

- Exercise design
- Participant recruitment
- Logistical organization
- Session moderation
- Output.

Exercise design
This is covered in the next chapter.

Participant recruitment
The output from a session depends on the participants. Identifying the competencies and experience that the participants must possess is vital

to the session's success. There may be only one type of participant – for example, neurologists – or more than one type – as in Project B, where there are both patients and caregivers. For each type of participant, you must define their number and parameters that describe their desired characteristics before recruitment can begin.

Logistical organization

This includes the location of the session, travel to the location for those who will attend, accommodation for those who need it and catering for the session (lunch and coffee breaks).

Session moderation

This is covered in a dedicated chapter later in the book.

Output

The result of every Collaborative Creativity session is recorded in a written document that also contains images of all the worksheets produced in the session.

At the end of a session the moderator must collect all the worksheets, any flip-chart sheets and of course the notes taken during the session. The notes should describe all the decisions and the main points of the conversations.

As a general rule, the notes of the moderator should be written up within 24 hours – if it is done later, the context and meaning of a hastily written note may be lost. When there is more than one moderator, they must always write up their notes separately, and within 48 hours of the conclusion of the session their notes should be compared and combined. These are then formatted into a document, complete with images of all the worksheets. Subsequently, the coach and the moderator conduct an analytical session to establish the relative importance of output items and, together, produce an executive summary – a short section of a document, usually placed at the beginning that summarizes the complete contents of the document – together with recommendations for the next steps based on the results and the given objective.

Before and after the session

Sometimes it is possible – indeed, even indispensable – to prepare or interrogate the participants in some way prior to a Collaborative Creativity session.

One example is an online survey, which can be used to get some simple questions out of the way, collect quantitative data about the participants or verify the group's opinion of a specific issue. The anonymous, aggregated results can be shared with the participants at the beginning of the session.

To get participants in the right frame of mind and to break the ice in a room of strangers, you can ask each participant to think of an example of something they have experienced, to present as a brief anecdote at the start of the session. Let's say the session will be focused on improving customer experience. You could ask participants to think of a great, or terrible, customer experience they have personally had and explain why it was special. You can collect the 'whys' from the anecdotes on a flip chart and use them as stimuli for a creative exercise.

If the participants are very engaged in the objective of the session, you can ask them to do some research on a specific topic to prime them with background information. If relevant information isn't readily available, or you want to provide specific intelligence, you can supply a short pre-read document to the participants.

Pre-work can also be more creative. A simple exercise that doesn't require particular tools is to ask participants to create a name or a mascot for a fictional new product or service that has some relevance to the objective of the session. In this case, creative pre-work is mental preparation because the tension of incomplete tasks is useful in creativity – it keeps us in a receptive state for solutions to ongoing problems allowing our subconscious to contemplate a problem even when we aren't consciously doing so.

Once a session is over, I strongly recommend keeping participants informed of progress on the project to which they've contributed. This is indispensable in certain situations – for instance, when a Collaborative Creativity session is focused on innovation or cohesion within a company and the participants are its employees. As we have seen previously, believing one's work is useful and valuable is a human need. The bare minimum of follow-up with participants is a communication thanking them for their participation.

After sessions focused on new ideas, the follow-up can also ask participants whether they have had any further thoughts – I call these 'next-day ideas'. A next-day idea is something that spontaneously pops into the mind while one is doing something else. Often I have heard from people who have had ideas on the train ride home from the session or in the shower the next morning (a cliché, I know, but it does happen). These ideas are always included in the session output document in a specific section clearly identified as post-session work. Following up with participants is also an opportunity to invite them to answer a short online survey (voluntary and anonymous) regarding their opinion of the session experience.

My personal preference is to always share the output document with participants, but the kind of information that can be found in this document is often sensitive and I understand the need to keep it confidential. On those occasions where the session is performed for a patient advocacy group, the results are usually made public as a white paper or, as we saw previously with PKU & ME, published in a scientific journal. When this is the case, it is important to keep participants informed of the output.

Further collaboration with groups of participants is, unfortunately, very rare. The 'Complete Co-Creation' approach described by Stefanie Jansen and Maarten Pieters[28] requires the participants and the sponsor to share the whole innovation process from start to finish. I find this interesting; however, in my experience this is an extremely problematic approach in the pharmaceutical healthcare sector – not least due to regulatory constraints.

A Collaborative Creativity session involving only the employees of a pharmaceutical company has the advantage of not being shackled by confidentiality or regulatory issues, and in these cases it is vital to use the momentum provided by the session and the positive energy of realization to push ahead with change. Co-authorship, co-ownership and pride in your work have a lingering effect only if something tangible is seen to emerge from the session. It is beneficial to make the Collaborative Creativity experience last and show it was not just a diversion – an amusing blip – but a durable change of course. The management and internal communication of projects is

---

[28] S. Jansen and M. Pieters, *The 7 Principles of Complete Co-Creation* (2018).

usually the responsibility of a client-side project manager, but the coach of a Collaborative Creativity project should provide assistance in describing progress and crediting the participants for the results achieved.

Collaborative Creativity exercises

Designing a specific set of exercises for a Collaborative Creativity session requires that the coach and also the client both think hard, up front, about the questions they want to ask and the exercises (basically a way of asking a question) that are most likely to inspire and produce useful results.

As you know by now, a Collaborative Creativity session contains more than one exercise. For simplicity, Figure 10 shows the flow of a single exercise.

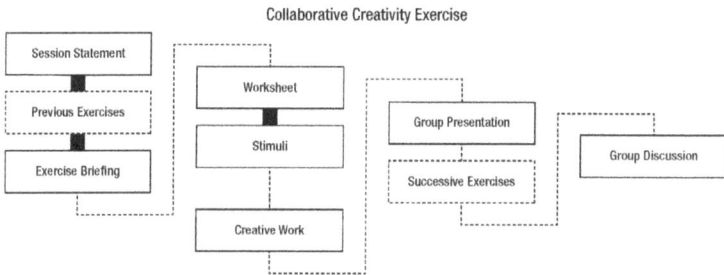

Figure 10: The flow of a single Collaborative Creativity exercise

From top left, the session statement is relevant because this is the session's purpose, which has engaged the participant; consequently, it provides context to all the exercises. Unless this is the first exercise in a session, you need to consider the influence of the previous exercises on the mindset of the participants. The exercise briefing is the moment when the moderator explains the exercise and the materials provided to the participants. The materials typically include a worksheet and some form of stimulus (we'll examine both in detail later). Creative work is the participants' creative activity on the exercise (usually in teams or individually). The group presentation of an exercise is when the participants share and comment on the work they have produced with the entire group of participants. Unless this is the last exercise, the successive exercises will be influenced by the ideas and mindset produced by the previous exercises and the cumulative effect will influence the group discussion that concludes the session.

Collaborative Creativity exercises are the engine that produces the five forces of Collaborative Creativity: they are the defining elements of a session and they allow a project to progress towards its objective.

Exercise design entails three things:

- curating the flow of the exercises in a session
- inventing the idea for each exercise
- designing the worksheets and stimuli.

Curating the flow of the exercises in a session

In a Collaborative Creativity session, there are multiple exercises. The sequence of creative exercises and the way different types of exercises are combined greatly influence the result of a session. Each exercise produces an output that on its own is valuable, and that increases when each exercise works synergistically with the other exercises towards an objective. A Collaborative Creativity session is an intellectual journey, the exercises are different stages of the journey and ultimately each stage must coherently contribute to reaching a destination.

Sometimes the influence of one exercise on another is only in the mindset that it creates in the participants. At other times the connection between the exercises is tangible, and the output from one becomes a stimulus for another. In both scenarios, the flow of a session needs to be considered carefully.

A tool I use for designing exercise flow is the session worksheet. Once again we can use the example from Project B – Figure 11 shows only the part dedicated to the exercises.

In this example, the session has four exercises. Time flows from left to right, so the exercise on the far left is the first and the one on the far right is the last.

You can clearly see that the first session is a team exercise, which aims to explore unmet needs and focuses on the forces of cohesion, empathy and self-discovery. This is followed by an individual exercise that aims to explore emotions and focuses firmly on self-discovery. The penultimate exercise is a team exercise that aims to identify practical help and that focuses on empathy and cohesion. The last exercise is another team exercise that aims to understand aspirations and focuses mainly on empathy.

The flow of this session begins with a simple exercise that allows the group to settle in, then an emotionally challenging individual exercise, followed by a more calm and practical exercise, and finally a challenging, aspirational and emotional exercise.

Remember that immediately following the last exercise the group discussion occurs. In this example, the flow is conducive to stimulating the participants' minds and creating the conditions for a lively and open conversation.

Compare this with the exercise flow in Figure 12, designed for an entirely different Collaborative Creativity session with a different objective for participants.

NEEDS	EMOTIONS	PRACTICAL HELP	HOPES
Question: NEEDS — What 3 things would you change regarding your condition?	**Question:** EMOTIONS — How does post-transplant health management make you feel? What's good + what's bad?	**Question:** PRACTICAL HELP — What services could help you manage your condition?	**Question:** HOPES — How do you see yourself and your condition in the future?
Single □ Team ☒ Group □	Single ☒ Team □ Group □	Single □ Team ☒ Group □	Single □ Team ☒ Group □
T-Prep: 10 T-Work: 40 T-Pres: 20	T-Prep: 5 T-Work: 20 T-Pres: 45	T-Prep: 5 T-Work: 50 T-Pres: 30	T-Prep: 5 T-Work: 40 T-Pres: 30
Exercise: Transforma	**Exercise:** Collage "Ups&Downs"	**Exercise:** Lifebelt	**Exercise:** Time travel
Materials: Transforma A3 worksheets, Blue marker pens	**Materials:** Black/white A3 worksheets, Scissors + tape	**Materials:** Prototype A2 worksheet, Blue marker pens + tape	**Materials:** Facebook page worksheet, Blue marker pens + tape
Stimuli: —	**Stimuli:** Colour photo magazines	**Stimuli:** Service option paper strips	**Stimuli:** —
Empathy ☆ ☆☆ ★★★ ☆☆☆ ☆☆☆☆ Realization ☆ ☆☆ ☆☆☆ ☆☆☆ ☆☆☆☆ Invention ☆ ☆☆ ☆☆☆ ☆☆☆ ☆☆☆☆ Cohesion ☆ ☆☆ ★★★ ☆☆☆ ☆☆☆☆ Self-discovery ☆ ☆☆ ★★★ ☆☆☆ ☆☆☆☆	Empathy ☆ ☆☆ ★★★ ☆☆☆ ☆☆☆☆ Realization ☆ ☆☆ ☆☆☆ ☆☆☆ ☆☆☆☆ Invention ☆ ☆☆ ☆☆☆ ☆☆☆ ☆☆☆☆ Cohesion ☆ ☆☆ ☆☆☆ ☆☆☆ ☆☆☆☆ Self-discovery ☆ ☆☆ ☆☆☆ ☆☆☆ ★★★★	Empathy ☆ ☆☆ ★★★ ☆☆☆ ☆☆☆☆ Realization ☆ ☆☆ ☆☆☆ ☆☆☆ ☆☆☆☆ Invention ☆ ☆☆ ★★★ ☆☆☆ ☆☆☆☆ Cohesion ☆ ☆☆ ★★★ ☆☆☆ ☆☆☆☆ Self-discovery ☆ ☆☆ ★★★ ☆☆☆ ☆☆☆☆	Empathy ☆ ☆☆ ★★★ ☆☆☆ ☆☆☆☆ Realization ☆ ☆☆ ☆☆☆ ☆☆☆ ☆☆☆☆ Invention ☆ ☆☆ ☆☆☆ ☆☆☆ ☆☆☆☆ Cohesion ☆ ☆☆ ★★★ ☆☆☆ ☆☆☆☆ Self-discovery ☆ ☆☆ ☆☆☆ ☆☆☆ ☆☆☆☆

Figure 11: Section of Project B worksheet dealing with the exercises

Question:	Question:	Question:	Question:
PATIENT EMPATHY	HCP EMPATHY	SERVICE DESIGN	DESIGN REFINE
What are the characteristics of the 3 main patient types?	How do HCPs typically approach the patient types?	Which is the most effective and efficient set of services?	How do we fit an optimal set of services into our integrated offering?
Single ☐ Team ☒ Group ☐	Single ☐ Team ☒ Group ☐	Single ☐ Team ☒ Group ☐	Single ☐ Team ☐ Group ☒
T-Prep: 20 T-Work: 30 T-Pres: 30	T-Prep: 20 T-Work: 30 T-Pres: 30	T-Prep: 5 T-Work: 40 T-Pres: 30	T-Prep: 5 T-Work: 60 T-Pres: –
Exercise:	Exercise:	Exercise:	Exercise:
Identikit for 3 patient types	Role play HCP with 3 patient types	Octopus (10 tentacles)	Octopus
Materials:	Materials:	Materials:	Materials:
3 Identikit worksheets Blue marker pens	3 patient-type worksheets Blue marker pens	Octopus A2 worksheet Blue marker pens + tape	Octopus A2 worksheet and post-it notes
Stimuli:	Stimuli:	Stimuli:	Stimuli:
Patient experience from patient CCS	HCP attitudes and beliefs from HCP CCS	Service options from HCP and patient CCS	Octopus worksheets from previous exercise
Empathy ☆ ☆☆ ☆☆☆ ★★★★★ Realization ☆ ☆☆ ☆☆☆ ☆☆☆ Invention ☆ ☆☆ ★★★★★ ☆☆☆ Cohesion ☆ ☆☆ ☆☆☆ ☆☆☆ Self-discovery ☆ ★★★ ☆☆☆ ☆☆☆	Empathy ☆ ☆☆ ☆☆☆ ★★★★★ Realization ☆ ☆☆ ☆☆☆ ☆☆☆ Invention ☆ ☆☆ ★★★★★ ☆☆☆ Cohesion ☆ ☆☆ ☆☆☆ ☆☆☆ Self-discovery ☆ ★★★ ☆☆☆ ☆☆☆	Empathy ☆ ☆☆ ☆☆☆ ★★★★★ Realization ☆ ☆☆ ★★★★★ ☆☆☆ Invention ☆ ☆☆ ☆☆☆ ☆☆☆ Cohesion ☆ ☆☆ ★★★★★ ☆☆☆ Self-discovery ☆ ☆☆ ☆☆☆ ☆☆☆	Empathy ☆ ☆☆ ☆☆☆ ☆☆☆ Realization ☆ ☆☆ ☆☆☆ ★★★★★ Invention ☆ ☆☆ ★★★★ ☆☆☆ Cohesion ☆ ☆☆ ★★★★★ ☆☆☆ Self-discovery ☆ ☆☆ ☆☆☆ ☆☆☆

Figure 12: Exercise flow

This example also has four exercises. You can clearly see that the first session is a team exercise, which aims to create an understanding of the patient and focuses mainly on empathy. The next exercise is also a team exercise focusing mainly on empathy, which aims to create an understanding of the healthcare practitioner. The penultimate exercise is the last team exercise and it aims to create practical ideas for service design and focuses on invention and cohesion. The last exercise is a group exercise that aims to create consensus in the whole group around a single idea; it focuses mainly on cohesion and realization.

The flow of this session begins with two team exercises that immerse the participants in the experience and mindset of different cohorts. This is followed by another team exercise in which participants use this knowledge to devise a practical service for these cohorts, and finally a group exercise that allows the participants to identify and combine the best ideas.

In this example, all the exercises are influenced by the work of others. At the beginning, the influence is derived from the output of previous sessions and at the end from the participants themselves. The flow is initially conducive to priming the participants with empathy that will help them produce relevant ideas, make informed decisions and then help them refine solutions as a cohesive group.

Inventing a creative exercise

The term 'garbage in, garbage out' (GIGO), comes from computer science. It has been credited to Wilf Hey, who invented it in 1965 while working at IBM. It neatly describes the rule that flawed, inappropriate or unintelligible input data will always produce output that is equally useless. The same principle applies to Collaborative Creativity: the quality of the exercises, worksheets and stimuli directly affect the quality of the output.

Good exercise design is about creating a well-defined, stimulating framework. An architect once told me that the essence of architecture isn't designing walls, windows and other features; rather, it is about designing the spaces defined by those tangible elements. Likewise, the job of the Collaborative Creativity coach is to design spaces for creativity to flourish. The exercises and worksheets are the walls and windows that define the spaces. Just as architecture defines different spaces for different building functions, a creative exercise must define different creative space for different objectives. While there are boundless applications of Collaborative Creativity, each of them uses different configurations of the five forces, so we will examine exercise design in the context of the forces.

Exercises for self-discovery

Self-discovery is essential to practical applications such as market research or internal reorganization. The aim of these types of creative exercises is to help the participants, individually and as a group, to examine their experience of a specific subject and reflect upon it honestly. Self-discovery occurs when someone becomes conscious of something that they weren't aware of previously; consequently, asking direct questions is not an ideal approach. Self-discovery requires oblique approaches that allow unconscious thoughts to emerge.

Exercises that use time travel require the participant to imagine the present from a different perspective, which can then reveal current beliefs. Exercises that ask the participant to think of ways in which someone else in their position would act can uncover incongruences between self and other. Exercises that use non-verbal expression, like collage, can allow a feeling to be expressed automatically and later examined.

Creative exercises for self-discovery subtly ask participants to reveal something about themselves, and the revelation is often equally subtle. What is revealed may be something that is omitted or something only slightly incongruous in a worksheet; the full significance becomes evident only when the participant has to explain it. In self-discovery, the presentation is even more important than the creation, and the questions and observations of the moderator are vital to help the subject realize the full significance of their work. A worksheet serves to expose a loose thread; it is only with conversation that the thread can be pulled and the insight fully unravelled.

To help identify the loose threads of incongruence, the moderator needs a point of reference. This is where multiple exercises are so valuable. By asking the participants to examine the same subject from different points of view, with different exercises, you are effectively hearing the same story multiple times in slightly different ways and from different perspectives. This makes it possible to spot not only similarities but also differences, and then to discuss these with the participants.

For the participants, talking with team-mates who share similar, albeit personal, experience can be enlightening and self-discovery can also stem from these discussions. However, the type of creative exercises that are most conducive to self-discovery are individual exercises.

A classic self-discovery sequence is to start with a simple team exercise to get everyone settled in and create a benchmark output, then immediately follow it with an individual exercise. This is preferable to scheduling the individual exercise later in the session because after various team exercises the mindset of the participants will be slightly less individualistic, having been influenced by the team-thinking of the previous exercises.

Exercises for empathy

Empathy is essential to practical applications such as market research, planning customer experiences and improving employee collaboration. The practical applications of empathy are of two types: *empathy out* and *empathy in*. Empathy out is where the members of a homogeneous group of participants examine and describe their common experience of a certain subject – for example, a disease, a professional role, a situation. Empathy in is where the members of a group of participants, which may be heterogeneous, learn about the specific experience of a cohort and apply this understanding to a practical aspect of their work – for example, physicians learning about patients or pharmaceutical marketers learning about prescribers.

In both cases, empathy borrows heavily from self-discovery, especially at the beginning of a session where the aim is to help insights emerge or for them to be absorbed. The two differ completely in how they continue: empathy out uses cohesion exercises to form a consensus on what a typical experience is like; empathy in uses invention exercises to apply the comprehension of the needs of others in a specific situation or activity in the creation of something new.

For empathy out, the aim of the creative exercises is to uncover useful insights about the cohort and then create a rich and coherent description of the participants' experience. Individual and team exercises of self-discovery that use time travel, third person or non-verbal expression all work well to uncover insights. Following these, you need team or group exercises like Lifebelt or Identikit (both of these are exercise formats described later on in the book), which help the cohort discover their commonalities.

For empathy in, the aim of the creative exercises is to comprehend useful insights about a cohort and then apply that knowledge to the creation of something new. To absorb empathy, team exercises that use role-playing work well – including exercises where the task is to imagine a situation in which you are someone else and you have to do something. Parallel universe (another exercise format described later on in the book) is one exercise that can help participants internalize information.

Sometimes, to transfer empathy you can use the same exercise in two different sessions. Let's say, for example, that you run two sessions: session 1, with patients as participants, is aimed at gathering insights, while session 2, with physicians, is aimed at understanding those insights. In session 1, among others, there is a Lifebelt exercise. In session 2, you can present a summary of the insights to the participants and have them perform the same Lifebelt exercise – when they have finished presenting their work, you can display the Lifebelt worksheets from session 1 and have the group compare the results.

Exercises for invention
All creative exercises are exercises for invention, even those not aimed specifically at finding new ideas. For the sake of clarity, I'm going to distinguish two main types of invention exercises with the names *explorative invention* and *practical invention*.

Take the session with the service design objective we looked at previously in this chapter. The first two exercises in that session required invention, yet that invention was focused on acquiring empathy for others. The output wasn't new ideas; it was new mindsets – this is explorative invention. Those two exercises allowed the next two exercises to produce a new empathy-based solution, but the output was a practical idea – this is practical invention.

Explorative invention uses creativity to reach means other than ideas. Dan Ariely writes:

> *I believe that recognizing where we depart from the ideal is an important part of the quest to truly understand ourselves, and one that promises many practical benefits. Understanding irrationality is important for our everyday actions and decisions, and for understanding how we design our environment and the choices it presents to us.*[29]

Explorative invention is a way to explore and understand irrationality. Exercises that use explorative invention are those used in self-discovery and empathy.

Practical invention is quite different. Here the output needs to speak for itself – it needs to be a new solution to the problem examined by the Collaborative Creativity session. In this case, the type of exercise – and the exercises leading up to it – must be designed precisely to frame the problem and inspire the participants.

It is important to understand that when you design a creative exercise for invention, you are designing a tool; however, you should not be defining what will be made with that tool. You are designing a process and an influential part of a process is its boundaries – for example, if you ask someone to design a biodegradable spoon, you have defined the outcome as a spoon-like object; if you ask them to design a solution for eating ice cream, the outcome might be the ice cream cone (in a world where the ice cream cone hasn't been invented yet).

The design of an exercise is one half of the framing; the other half is the stimulus you provide. Together, these two things will influence the ideas that are produced.

Exercises for cohesion

Cohesion is essential to practical applications such as corporate organization and culture, change management and market research. The aim of these types of creative exercise is to help a group of participants to understand each other and develop a point of view that they all identify with and support. Cohesion requires approaches that encourage unity and reciprocal understanding.

Sometimes cohesion is as simple as making sure everyone has the same information or shares an empathetic point of view regarding

---

[29] D. Ariely, *Predictably Irrational* (2010).

a certain cohort. Again, stimuli are influential as is the way you organize collaboration in an exercise.

The flow of the exercises is important, before you propose an exercise that aims to create consensus it is often a good idea to use exercises that highlight the existing differences and commonalities that exist in the group. This allows diversity to be expressed and understood before forging ahead and searching for homogeneity.

Transitioning from individual exercises, to small teams, then to larger teams and finally the full group is also a kind of flow that can be conducive to gradually creating cohesion, especially in sessions with heterogeneous participants.

In some cases a cohesion exercise can propose a mental model for a group to adopt in reaching consensus. A mental model is a description of a thought process about how something works and a mental model can define an approach to solving problems and performing tasks.[30]

The opening words of The Great Mental Models, Volume 2: Physics, Chemistry and Biology by Shane Parrish state that, 'The quality of your thinking depends on the mental models that are in your head.'

A united group is one that shares mental models and uses them to work together and solve problems together. The mental models can originate from corporate processes, third party models or be designed specifically for the occasion. Creative exercises that supply a mental model and allow a group to experiment with it are typical cohesion exercises.

Exercises for realization

Realization is essential to practical applications such as team building, employee motivation and customer experience. Realization is a secondary product of all successful creative exercises. I don't think an exercise can be designed to produce only realization because realization is dependent on the successful completion of a task. Realization is spontaneously achieved through invention, self-discovery, cohesion and empathy, so if your main objective is realization, my advice is

---

[30] For more information on mental models, I recommend an excellent article, 'Mental Models: The Best Way to Make Intelligent Decisions (109 Models Explained)', on the Farnam Street website: https://fs.blog/mental-models.

to identify a project that focuses on one of these and kill two birds with one stone.

That said, there are things you can do to ensure that a Collaborative Creativity session is rewarding:

- Make sure the objective of the session is considered purposeful and valuable by the participants.

- Push participants to achieve the best result possible, but don't exaggerate and make the experience stressful.

- Remember that creative energy lasts between 20 and 40 minutes, so respect people's energy.

- Make clear what happens to the work, and keep post-session communication (and where appropriate involvement) open to show the concrete application of the session output.

Finally, always try to make the exercises fun. Creativity is a kind of play – it is the brain having fun. The tone and style of the exercise and worksheet should always be appropriate for the participants and conducive to letting their brains have fun. As George Bernard Shaw once said, 'We don't stop playing because we grow old; we grow old because we stop playing.'

Designing the worksheet and stimuli

Each exercise should have a worksheet, or a set of worksheets. A worksheet is a tool and the way it is designed also affects the exercise. Its constraints influence the work produced – for example, if the worksheet provides, for a certain item, a small space (and this is accompanied with a thick marker), you will force the user to choose only a few words or draw a very simple figure. This affects the time that will be spent on this item and also encourages prioritization and simplicity. On the contrary, a figure surrounded by 12 large, empty call-out boxes creates an expectation of diverse and detailed responses.

The size of a worksheet also creates an expectation. Worksheets can be any size – I tend to use three standard sizes: small, which is A3; medium, which is 35 x 50 cm; and large, which is 50 x 70 cm. Small works best for individual exercises or team exercises where multiple solutions will be produced, each on a separate worksheet.

Medium is the typical format for simple team exercises and large is used for more complex team or group exercises.

Taking the time and the ingenuity to create a good-looking worksheet can really make a difference in terms of the efficacy of the exercise as appropriate stimulation for various reasons:

- A tool that has obviously been specifically designed for a task is like a creative benchmark that invites reciprocal care and effort.

- The more relevant the information and images on the worksheet are to the participants, the more they will feel engaged in the exercise.

- The spaces designed on the worksheet for different parts of the answer help to guide participants' thinking and time management.

A well-designed worksheet also provides a standard means of presentation of ideas that:

- makes it easy to compare different worksheets because the component parts of an idea are always expressed in the same place
- divides and defines the components of an idea equally for all the teams, which makes it easy to mix and match components from different worksheets (in a subsequent phase or exercise)
- reduces 'presentation anxiety' because the worksheet format provides a degree of visual uniformity and elegance to even the scruffiest of work
- is slightly less intimidating than a blank piece of paper.

Regarding style, you are free to use whatever you consider appropriate. My preference is usually for cartoon drawings or simple graphic icons to represent something because it looks simple and informal, and allows subjective interpretation.

You should always consider very carefully any stimuli you provide for an exercise because the content and tone of the stimuli will guide and influence the output.

My attitude to stimuli is that less is more and none is best. In other words, if an exercise can be designed to elicit a response without stimuli, this is usually preferable.

Let's consider the main types of stimuli:

- external qualitative (empathy) stimuli
- external 'provocative' stimuli
- internal stimuli.

External qualitative stimuli include things like the description of patient attitudes and needs. These should be summarized so they convey only the key points that are pertinent to the exercise and, when possible, they should be 'humanized' with direct quotes.

I use these types of stimuli when they are indispensable for the participants' comprehension of a point of view they may otherwise lack.

External provocative stimuli are things that are provided to gain a reaction. Sometimes some pertinent work might have been done previously and there can be a temptation to expose the participants to aspects of it. I generally oppose this for various reasons: they stimulate critical thought, which I believe contrasts with creative thought; they can be too influential and easily skew an outcome; and they are often a list of preconceptions or a collection of pre-existing ideas that might be better investigated using other methods.

Sometimes, though, provocative stimuli are indispensable. When this is the case, I suggest mixing random or 'wrong' items with the 'serious' stimuli. I think people instinctively recognize a selection of related items and consequently consider each item in comparative terms, whereas if they perceive a seemingly random set of items, their reaction to each will be more objective.

Internal stimuli are things created within the session or prior to the session by the participants themselves. These are the only type of stimuli I employ enthusiastically in sessions, but even here I limit use to where it is appropriate – where an iterative, constructive approach is beneficial to the session objective.

Collaborative Creativity exercise formats

As one of the principles of Collaborative Creativity states, exercises are unique to each project. This means they need to be designed specifically. However, I have found particular exercise formats to be extremely flexible, allowing all kinds of personalization. The following are seven examples of formats that work well and can be adapted to a wide range of situations (more exercise formats are available on my website, at https://peter-comber.net/collaborativecreativity). Each exercise format description includes a few examples that explain how the exercise can be personalized, to get you started. Ultimately, I hope they inspire you to create your own exercises.

Time travel

Useful for: understanding a group's experience of positive and negative change, understanding a group's hopes/fears for the future (and from this their current sensitivities), understanding priorities of needs.

Very good for: self-discovery, empathy, invention, cohesion.

Good for: realization.

Type of exercise: individual or team.

General description

Any exercise that invites a group to look into the past or imagine the future fits into this category. Looking at the past or future is a great way to get people to examine specific aspects of their present situation. At the heart of this kind of exercise is comparison. Participants have to consider the present and some other time, and compare them. The focus you give to the exercise will obviously determine what they focus on, so this exercise can be tailored to examine very specific aspects, very general things or anything in between. It is, however, important to indicate how many things you want them to list because this creates a minimum expectation and implicitly asks them to prioritize – if you ask for three things, the participants have to decide which top three things are the most important or relevant. Another variable that can be used to calibrate the exercise is the recipient of the message from the past or future: the self works best for patients/caregivers and occasionally physicians; peers works well with physicians and corporate colleagues; while third parties work with all participants.

Requirements

A worksheet with a visual theme that reflects the projected date of the assignment and plenty of space for the participants to write notes. This type of exercise doesn't require a particular stimulus.

Example assignments

- 'A new feature on your phone allows you to send a text message back in time X years to yourself. What five things would you tell your younger self to do differently regarding ZXY (subject)?' The worksheet could be a large drawing of a smartphone with space to write within the message app (the length of the message is a variable you can play with).

- 'Your team will go back in time for a medical congress. As specialists of the future, you must make a speech describing to your colleagues how their practice will change over the next X years. List the top three positive and top three negative things you think they should know await them.' The worksheet could be a mock-up agenda of a symposium of a medical congress that really took place in the past, with spaces to write the names of the speakers and their main talking points.

- 'You have a telescope that looks into the future. When you look at ZXY (subject: it could be their clinical practice for healthcare practitioners; a patient's quality of life for caregivers; their product/service for clients), what do you see?' The worksheet could have an illustration of a telescope running across the top and below it three or four moleskin-style notebook pages to write on with 'Observations' as a heading. The number of pages indicates your expectation of the number of observations you would like the participants to imagine.
- 'Thinking of X years ago, what are the five things you are most nostalgic about regarding X (subject: condition, clinical practice, brand) and the five things you are most thankful have changed?' The worksheet could have an illustration of a pair of scales (one plate 'nostalgic' and the other 'grateful') with space above the two plates in which to write the two sets of five things.

Outcome

When reviewing the outcome, it is vital to look at what is omitted as well as what is included and ask why something didn't make the list because sometimes the things that don't make the list reveal more about opinions, beliefs and experience than those that do.

Lifebelt

Useful for: understanding a group's needs and desires, understanding a group's beliefs regarding the needs and desires of another, diverse group.

Very good for: empathy, invention, realization, cohesion.

Good for: self-discovery.

Type of exercise: team.

General description

This category includes exercises where the participants consider a situation/condition by focusing on advice they would give someone in a given situation. A lifebelt is a useful metaphor – it is associated with helping and saving others – but the object can be anything your imagination suggests or that is appropriate for the cohort/objective.

This kind of exercise asks the participants to design an object with special features that are useful to a specific type of person or situation – it is useful for quickly understanding participants' opinions about and knowledge of a certain subject. When the participants are not part of the group of people for whom the object is designed, it becomes an exercise in empathy. When the participant is one of the people for whom the object is designed, it is an exercise in self-discovery that allows them to talk about their own needs and desires in the third person.

Requirements

A worksheet with a visual theme that reflects the assignment and plenty of space for the participants to write notes. Generally speaking, this type of exercise works best towards the end of a session when the participants have been working on the subject for a while and they can draw – at least in part – on the output of previous exercises for inspiration.

Example assignments

- 'Create a lifebelt for XZY (type of person) to help them ZXY (the objective).' The worksheet could be a large drawing of a lifebelt with four segments (each representing a different type of help) and space to write in.

- 'Create a shop for XZY (type of person). What are the features that make it perfect for them? What kinds of articles does it sell? What services does it provide? When is it open?' The worksheet could be a big sketch of a shop to be completed by drawing content with captions.

- 'Create a personal robot for XYZ (type of person). What does the robot know? What can it do? What tools can it use? When is it useful and why?' The worksheet could be a large drawing of a robot with empty captions indicating various parts to write in (more caption spaces, more characteristics).

- 'Create the perfect holiday for XZY (type of person). What kind of holiday is it? What location? What activities? What amenities and services? What companions?' The worksheet could be the two mostly empty sides of a picture postcard to be completed – one part image and the other part written description of the characteristics of the holiday.

Outcome

When reviewing the outcome, you must try to understand (and help the participant understand) why something is considered valuable and the problem it solves, not just how it solves it.

Transforma

Useful for: understanding the pain points or aspirations of an individual or group.

Very good for: self-discovery, empathy, cohesion.

Good for: invention.

Type of exercise: individual or team.

General description

This type of exercise includes all those where the participants are given the power to change something with the help of an imaginary and extraordinary power, device or being. The Transforma can be anything you like. I frequently use an illustration of a fantastic steam contraption with a steampunk aesthetic. There is a funnel on the left side of the machine and a big box on a conveyor belt exiting the machine. The participants have to write on the funnel the thing they would like to change and write on the box how they would like it to change. Obviously you have to establish limits to the Transforma's powers, and this is one of the variables you can control. If, for example, the participants are patients, the Transforma will not be able to eliminate their illness (or will it? – your decision). Ask them to be specific about the changes, as the Transforma doesn't understand vague changes. They can make as many specific changes as they like in the time given, each on a different worksheet. These kinds of exercise are commonly used at the beginning of a session to allow a group to immediately express their frustrations and you can use successive exercises to fix the issues that emerge in the Transforma exercise. This kind of exercise is usually very productive and cathartic, so supply lots of worksheets.

Requirements

A worksheet with a visual theme that reflects either the subject of the assignment or the means of transformation and two large spaces for describing the before and after. This type of exercise doesn't require any particular stimulus.

Example assignments

- 'The Transforma can modify, one at a time, specific aspects of your clinical practice regarding ZXY (disease type) patients. What changes do you request?' The worksheet could be a large drawing of a Transforma machine.

- 'You have the power to create special sunglasses that can change other people's perception of your disease. What changes do you ask for?' The worksheet could be a large drawing of a pair of sunglasses and the change can be written directly onto the lenses of the glasses – maybe differentiating types of change with the two lenses.

- 'The Transforma can modify, one at a time, specific beliefs of your customers. What beliefs would you change and how?' The worksheet could be a large drawing of a Transforma machine with a physician wired up to it (it's not unethical, it's fun!) and two empty screens on which the participants can describe the before and after.

- 'You have found Aladdin's lamp and the genie grants you three wishes, but his powers are limited to YXZ (subject). What are the three wishes?' The worksheet could be a large drawing of a genie holding out his three hands (he's a genie, he can have as many hands as you want him to have!) palm upwards. The space above the hands is where the participants can describe the three wishes.

Outcome

The outcome of this exercise is usually very straightforward. Usually the thing to be changed is much more interesting than its transformation, so it is prudent to plan subsequent exercises where participants can probe deeper into the issues. The only other thing to watch out for are any problems of which you are aware that aren't subjected to the Transforma. As usual, just ask why not.

Collage

Useful for: understanding an individual's emotions about something.

Very good for: self-discovery, empathy, cohesion.

Good for: realization.
Type of exercise: individual.

General description

In this kind of exercise, participants look at a random collection of images in a search for something that represents, in some way, the feelings they have about a given subject. The most important thing for this exercise is to ensure freedom of expression and spontaneity. Because of this, I always tell participants that, if they prefer they can sketch and write something, but they should still select at least one photo (or more) from the magazines. The reason is simple: there is a difference between thinking about what you want to convey and using a drawing or words to describe it, and having a reaction to a random image. The sketch and words are controlled; the reaction to the random image is (when the exercise is done correctly) subconscious. Once the person has seen an image and felt a reaction, they need to understand why they reacted to it. That process of elaboration, understanding the relationship that the image has with the participant's experience of the subject, is the key to gleaning emotional insights.

A variation of the collage is the 'choose a postcard' exercise. I have a collection of over 200 postcard-size printed colour images. The subject and the style of the images varies wildly. I cover a table with the postcards, image side up, and ask the participants to select one postcard that they find resonates with the subject I have given them. When everyone has a postcard, the participants take it in turns to show their chosen image and explain their choice. This is much faster and easier for the participants because it is less probing than a collage, but it still produces useful results.

Requirements

A worksheet that forms a frame for the collage and many colour magazines of various types and themes with lots of photographs. To keep the responses uniquely representative of each individual, it is best to perform this exercise towards the beginning of the session. However, for best results you need to have established that the session is a safe place, so I usually place this as the second exercise. I always supply an abundance of colour magazines containing many photographs, together with scissors and tape. The worksheet usually depicts an empty picture frame with the title of the picture (the object of the exercise) written on the frame. When there are two subjects, the worksheet depicts a double picture frame, with each frame having a title.

Example assignments

- 'Create a collage depicting how you feel about ZYX (a specific situation – for example, in the clinic when you forget to take medication).' The worksheet could be a picture frame (have fun choosing a suitable style) with the title of the picture (also the name of the exercise) written on the frame.

- 'Create a collage depicting yourself as a XYZ (the role we are interested in, for example: caregiver, physician, patient).' The worksheet could be a drawing of a hand holding a mirror; the empty space inside is for the collage.

- 'Create two collages, one depicting your emotions towards XYZ (the disease) and the other depicting yourself.' The worksheet could be a double picture frame with the title of the two pictures written on the frames.

- 'Create two collages, one depicting the things that give you strength and the other depicting the things that take away your energy (or motivation) regarding managing XYZ (the disease).' The worksheet could be two drawings of smartphones side by side, one with a full battery icon, the other with an exhausted battery icon. The screens of the two phones are the empty space for the collage.

Outcome

In this exercise, the participants' interpretation of the image and the meaning they attribute to the composition when they present it are much more important than the finished worksheet. Often in a collage exercise, an important image will be incorporated but not spontaneously commented upon when presented. Look out for this and ask about it.

Identikit

Useful for: understanding the emotions/characteristics of a group regarding a given subject or to generate empathy in a group towards a certain type of person.

Very good for: empathy, realization, cohesion.

Good for: invention.

Type of exercise: team.

General description

There are various kinds of identikit exercises. One kind is the *archetype exercise* where the object is to describe the common characteristics of a certain kind of person. Sometimes a single generalization is impossible or undesirable, however, and in these cases you can ask a team to identify two or three kinds of archetypes that can usefully describe a certain category of people (for example this could be a physician type, conservative/prudent and progressive/aggressive or patient type, with comorbidities and without comorbidities). These types of exercise are useful for understanding the beliefs and experience of the participant group with another group, or for focusing the participant group on the mindset of another group.

Sphere of influence is another kind of identikit exercise that can be used to map the external influences of a given subject. The idea is to create a sort of Venn diagram with a representation of the type of person that is the subject in the centre and various circles around them. The participants' task is to describe the circles of influence relevant to the subject (people, situations, institutions, information media, etc.). The detail of the type of influence or the relevant spheres are things you can calibrate in accordance with the objectives of the session.

A third type of identikit exercise is *anthropomorphization*. Anthropomorphism is the attribution of human characteristics to non-human subjects and it is an innate tendency of human psychology. It can be a very effective tool for learning the emotions attached to an experience – for example, you can ask a group to create an animal/monster to represent their experience of a certain disease or brand.

Requirements

A worksheet with some kind of representation of a human and plenty of space for personalization. The archetype kind of exercise can employ named captions to direct the thinking of the participants to specific characteristics and even be accompanied by stimuli from previous qualitative or quantitative research and other scientific literature. Archetype and spheres of influence identikit exercises are usually most useful at the beginning of a session; once these have been created, they can become a reference for successive exercises. Anthropomorphic identikit exercises are best used immediately before an exercise like Transforma so that fears can be addressed in some way by the participants.

Example assignments

- 'Describe ZXY (subject) as an animal/monster. What sex is it? What kind of (super)powers does it have? What does it look like? What kinds of habits and habitat does it favour? What kind of character and emotions does it project?' The worksheet could show a large cage and be accompanied by a bag of 'parts' with which to construct an animal/monster (with captions that describe it).

- 'Define the key similarities and differences of compliant and non-compliant patients with YXZ (subject).' The worksheet could be a sketch of two very similar people with empty captions for both to be completed.

- 'Identify and describe the sources that influence the XYZ's (subject) knowledge/beliefs regarding their clinical practice.' The worksheet could be a simple sketch of a physician surrounded by circles that participants can name and fill with notes.

- 'Create three archetypes for ZYX (subject). For each archetype, define what attitude they have, what they believe and how they act. What do they have in common and what makes them different? What else do we know that makes the archetypes different?' The worksheet could contain sketches of three people, each with an empty space for writing a description.

Outcome

When reviewing the main thing is to look for congruence and incongruence in the different teams' worksheets, use group conversation to understand origin and importance of the diversity among worksheets.

Parallel universe

Useful for: producing new ideas or for gathering insights about a cohort's experience of some specific thing.

Very good for: self-discovery, empathy, invention.

Good for: realization, cohesion.

Type of exercise: team or individual.

General description

These kinds of exercise propose an imaginary place where everything is the same as the world the participants live in except for one (or more) thing that is different. This could be something missing, something added or something that acts differently – obviously the thing, or things, you change are pertinent to the objective of the session.

These kinds of exercise ask participants to rethink things they take for granted. Almost anything that asks, 'What if…' fits into this category.

This exercise is particularly revealing when the participants are a heterogeneous group and can be formed into homogeneous teams, the different points of view of different cohorts is highlighted in their diverse interpretations of the proposed change.

It is also a great innovation exercise as it can produce highly unusual ideas.

Requirements

A worksheet that describes/visualizes that which is different in the parallel universe and provides space, or spaces, where the consequences of this can be noted. Multiple spaces with captions can invite reflections on the effects of the change on specific things or people.

Example assignments

- 'In a parallel universe, you can remotely control your patients for exactly 120 seconds every day, how do you use this time?' The worksheet could be an elaborate remote control machine that needs to be programmed with time, action, etc.

- 'In a parallel universe, you can be in two places at once for 10 minutes every day, how do you use this time?' The worksheet could be a double calendar entry.

- 'In a parallel universe, everybody is absolutely convinced of XXX and YYY, how does this affect ZZZ?' Or the opposite: 'In a parallel universe, nobody believes XXX and YYY, how does this affect ZZZ?'

- 'In a parallel universe, people don't have mouths or digestive tracts. How do you administer drug X?' The worksheet could show a drug packaging to be completed with the formulation and next to it a prescription to be written out.

Outcome

When presenting, teams correctly tend to explain only the alternative reality they have imagined, sometimes it is important to ask how this differs from today and maybe ask why certain positive changes can't be implemented in our universe.

As usual, look out for congruence and incongruence in the different teams' worksheets, use group conversation to explore the significance and importance of the diversity.

Pre-session exercises

Collaborative Creativity sessions are always very productive, yet sometimes when we are planning we realize we need to do even more and there simply isn't enough time. A possible solution is a pre-session exercise: a simple task for the Collaborative Creativity session participants, on which they are invited to work prior to the session. There are many options and valid reasons for doing this, but first I want to examine when it is appropriate because the first variable to consider is the participants. We must always remember to be grateful to those who commit to participating in a Collaborative Creativity session and never take advantage of their availability. If a pre-session exercise is to be part of the session, the participant must be aware of it when they are being recruited.

With the exception of a simple online survey to verify that they are appropriate candidates, I have never used a pre-session exercise with patients or caregivers. I don't wish to impose and I want to avoid any source of anxiety or potential misunderstanding. With physicians, however, a pre-session exercise can be both useful and appropriate. A Collaborative Creativity session with client staff as participants is the context in which I find pre-session exercises most useful.

Pre-session exercises can be used to ask participants to release any pent up ideas and preconceptions; start thinking about something or noticing something they don't normally think about; or identify positive examples of something. The exercise could be a survey that can form a baseline measuring knowledge or attitude. It could be a request to create a list of positive and negative aspects of a given subject. The results of these kinds of information gathering can be presented at the beginning of the Collaborative Creativity session as a measurement of the group's current state, as proof of a shared belief or as evidence of an issue to react against. Information gathering is a simple exercise, but other more ambitious tasks are possible and sometimes desirable.

It can be useful to get participants to think about something specific before the session. If, for example, the objective of the session is to improve an aspect of the company's operations, you can ask each participant to think of an example of a personal experience they have had with a brand outside their industry that excels in that aspect. If there is an emotional focus, then an exercise that makes them think about a particular emotion is very useful. For example, you can ask participants to write a haiku about that emotion or describe an object/place/person that in some way evokes the emotion. When there is a particular subject that is strongly related to the objective, it is sometimes a good idea to ask participants to write a short description of their opinion of the subject – you can, for example, provide the beginning of three or four sentences and ask each participant to complete the sentences.

These kinds of 'homework' exercises can then be presented at the very beginning of the session. When the group of participants includes colleagues who have never met before – which can happen in international multidisciplinary meetings – the initial round-the-table introduction can be less formal when each person introduces not just themselves but also their homework. This can be particularly useful if there are people of different levels of seniority participating, as it immediately makes a formal business ritual more playful, providing a good introduction to a Collaborative Creativity session.

Something that should always be avoided is asking directly for solutions to the main objective of the session. When participants arrive with ideas they think are viable and valuable, it can block the creativity of the session as they are then tempted to try to stick with their original solution instead of inventing new things. It can also be a source of conflict between participants as they protect 'their' ideas – an idea created by an individual before the session negates any possibility of a co-ownership effect. Another task that can be potentially toxic is asking for examples (positive or negative) that refer directly to the activities of the company where the participants work. It is always best to look outside the company and its industry for examples and inspiration.

Moderating

Recruiting a great group of participants and designing fantastic exercises is futile if the session is then poorly moderated. This chapter provides advice on how to moderate effectively and examines the role of the moderator before, during and after a session.

Preparation

The coach who designs a session and the person who moderates it can be the same person or different people. When they are different people, the first task of a moderator is to be briefed by the coach on the session objective, design and participants. Once this is done, the session becomes the responsibility of the moderator.

The moderator is also responsible for deciding how many additional moderators are required for the session and identifying and coordinating them.

One of the first things to do is carefully study the exercises and materials, to then produce a detailed agenda with estimated start and end times for each activity. This allows the moderator to check that the agenda provided by the coach has realistic allotted times and it will also help the moderator to track time during the session.

Carefully planning an agenda means always knowing what should be happening, but a good moderator doesn't blindly follow the agenda

– if a very interesting and valuable conversation is taking place during an exercise presentation it would be wrong to cut it off just to respect a timetable. Flexibility and adaptability are important, so when it is necessary to adapt the agenda and its timing, a moderator must be ready with options and a clear understanding of priorities and objectives.

The moderator is responsible for deciding the composition of the teams. The participants are provided by the recruiter and the coach's session design defines how many teams are needed and how many people will be in each team. The moderator must collaborate with the coach and recruiter to decide the team into which each person will be placed.

For example, authority is a characteristic of the participants that should be carefully considered when there are professionals of different levels of seniority or prestige. The way they are mixed or separated can have a significant effect on output and also the general mood of the session. Suppose you have three very senior people and six junior people. If the objective is to produce original ideas, I would recommend one team with all three seniors and two teams of three juniors each. If the objective is integration and optimization, then three teams with one senior and two juniors each is a better configuration.

I recommend creating a slide deck for the session. This should contain only a few slides to support, in writing, the things that must be explained clearly to the group – for example, the session statement, the composition of the teams, a summary of the briefing for each exercise and the session rules. You can download a set of standard session rules from my website at https://peter-comber.net/collaborativecreativity.

Once all this has been done, all that remains is to collect everything that is needed for the session (worksheets, stimuli, name tags, pens, scissors, tape, etc.), because it is the moderator's responsibility to ensure that all materials arrive safely at the session location.

Session moderation

Session moderation is 33% time management, 33% tone management, 33% wilful ignorance and 1% acting as a catalyst. Moderation is the ability and the willingness to let others shine. A moderator should be in control but never controlling. A moderator is both an indispensable facilitator and a vacuum. A moderator promotes the self-expression, conversation and creativity of others.

33% time management

The most basic ability of a moderator is to keep things moving. Good time management is not precise adherence to the times indicated on the agenda; on the contrary, it is the ability to extract the maximum value from the total amount of time given. The agenda is a planning tool, not an inviolable schedule. But deviating from the agenda requires awareness of the priorities and objectives of the session and a firm understanding of what has already been achieved in the session and what can still be achieved in the time remaining.

For example, during the presentation of an exercise, a conversation spontaneously arises on a subject that you know to be a priority. The right thing to do is let the conversation run its course; the wrong thing is to cut it off to stay on schedule, then later try to revive the conversation in the group discussion at the end of the session. In another example, during the presentation of an exercise a subject pops up that is not pertinent to the objective of the session and sparks a discussion. In this case, the wrong thing to do is let it run its course and the right thing to do is to cut off the discussion by respectfully writing a description of the subject on a flip-chart and informing the group that it will be covered in the group discussion at the end of the session. These are important decisions that influence the focus of the group at any given time, but they don't influence what the group thinks. This is what I mean by being in control but not controlling.

Time management is being realistic and knowing where value lies. A moderator should always walk around the room to monitor (and eavesdrop on) the progress of exercises; if an exercise looks nearly complete before time, ask the participants whether they are happy to finish a few minutes early or if you feel they need more time, offer it.

The greatest caution in time management must be used during worksheet presentations. Generally speaking, when individuals or teams present what they say and how they say it is more important than the content of the worksheet itself. Moderators should listen carefully, take notes and minimize interruptions. The occasional question to clarify something is fine. Brief encouraging comments are recommended, especially for people who are unused to presenting, because making people explain an idea to a lifeless and expressionless audience is a form of torture and contradicts the Collaborative Creativity principle of ensuring a safe and stimulating environment. A good moderator facilitates the flow and keeps the group focused on the objective.

33% tone management

Tone management is the ability to create and maintain a desired atmosphere in the room. As host, the moderator sets the tone for the session. An informal environment is conducive to creativity and collaboration, but it is important to maintain a professional atmosphere. It requires equilibrium: a Collaborative Creativity session may be fun, but first of all it is work.

Certain conditions are conducive to being creative and sharing personal thoughts and it is the moderator's responsibility to provide those conditions. How to do this and how effective you are is a question of individual sensitivity and requires emotional intelligence. The attitude and actions (verbal and non-verbal) of the moderator communicate to the group an attitude and mood, and under normal conditions the group will respond to this. There is no standard approach – it must be tailored to the group of participants and it is a continuous process that must adapt to the evolution of the group dynamic over time.

For example, in a Collaborative Creativity session with a group of adult patients, the start of the session is often awkward, as the members of the group are all complete strangers in an unfamiliar environment. The moderator's attitude must be calming, welcoming and reassuring. The objective is to make people comfortable, and to create an informal and non-judgemental vibe. You should aim to boost the confidence of the group and try to imply the bond that people with a shared experience can feel – tell them that they are all experts, and that their individual experience with their condition makes them uniquely qualified as a group to do the work today. Tell them that the exercises will help them, even when they are challenged by them – especially when they are challenged by them. If you are successful, after a while the group members will begin to familiarize with each other, become more relaxed and possibly start joking around. This is very positive because it creates a good atmosphere, but it is also potentially negative because the trajectory the group is on is becoming increasingly relaxed and informal. It is up to the moderator to keep them from degenerating into an uncontrolled mob. So if necessary, remind them of the seriousness of the objective to keep them focused on the task.

The end of a session is a bitter-sweet occasion. If it has been a good experience – possibly even cathartic – the fact that it is over can be a bit melancholy. As Priya Parker points out, 'It is your job as a gatherer to create an intentional closing that helps people face, rather than avoid, the end.'[31] Express gratitude, convey to participants the value to you of the work they have done, ask them to look at all the worksheets hanging on the wall, make sure they leave with a sense of accomplishment.

Different types of groups pose very different challenges. Caregivers are often human volcanoes of emotions and require extreme delicacy and tact. Physicians tend to present themselves as the opposite: they are extremely professional, emotionally contained and the objective is to give them permission to reveal their humanity and not just interpret their professional role. Internal sessions with client staff pose a different challenge because of pre-existing relationships in the group – a situation that can also arise in certain groups of healthcare providers, especially specialists of rare diseases who tend to know each other. In these cases, the focus of the moderator's effort is not towards creating an *esprit de corps* but rather establishing a sort of temporary autonomous zone – a space where the usual hierarchies, frictions and relational mechanisms are suspended and an unusual freedom can be explored and expressed.

33% wilful ignorance

If a moderator is in control of time and tone, they are correctly exercising power and authority. If that moderator also demonstrates expertise and knowledge on the subject of the session, then they are an influencer, not a moderator. For the duration of the session as a moderator, you must silence your ego and any desire to appear knowledgeable on the subject of the session. A moderator has no

---

[31] P. Parker, *The Art of Gathering: How We Meet and Why It Matters* (2018).

solutions, only questions. A moderator doesn't jump to conclusions – doesn't ever put words in people's mouths. Strive to be aware of your own preconceptions, otherwise you will see and hear what you want and expect to see and hear. A moderator should aspire to temporary ignorance for the duration of the session.

Ask participants to explain any jargon and industry-specific concepts they use. Sometimes people agree on a sentence but their individual interpretation of certain words or concepts within it is different and in reality their understanding of the meaning of the sentence is contrasting and their underlying beliefs are not aligned.

Make sure there is agreement on the definition and comprehension of important things. If the members of a group don't share the same meanings of their language, their discussions are meaningless. The same is true of concepts. Take, for example, an idea like transparency. A group might all agree on the importance of transparency, but what does it mean in the context of the session? If you investigate, you might discover that while there is agreement about the idea of transparency, opinions on how that translates into reality and actions might be very different. If you think there might be any doubt about the interpretation of a concept, ask for examples and definitions.

Don't worry about seeming naïve. If you expect people to expose their doubts and to share their insecurity, you must lead by example and ask 'dumb' questions. You are the outsider, so use that status to challenge and investigate the group's assumptions. You can usually tell when your dumb question has struck a nerve. If everyone still looks at you after you've finished asking the question, they probably consider the question genuinely dumb. If everyone starts looking at everyone else or (tellingly) someone in particular, then they too are curious to hear the answer to that question; you have struck a nerve with a not-so-dumb question.

In certain situations – especially with corporate groups – the role of the moderator is almost like that of the jester in a mediaeval court: you can question things others don't dare to. Ask questions like a child. You know how children repeatedly ask 'Why?' Do that, but without being annoying and obtuse. In the right context, 'Why?' can be a very powerful question. When you get to the point where people can't describe why they do something, you have probably found something interesting.

Children are also good at asking awkward and embarrassing questions, so channel your inner child and go for it. As a moderator, your duty is always to protect and respect your participants while achieving the objective that you have promised your client. Especially with patients and caregivers, you should always be careful to not upset or offend anyone. However, the insights you gather will be superficial if you don't do a bit of digging and there is an interesting piece of research that suggests you are probably more uncomfortable asking certain questions than the person you are asking. The research has a great title: 'I Didn't Want to Offend You: The Cost of Avoiding Sensitive Questions.'[32] It contains the following passage:

> People hate asking sensitive questions. However, it turns out that people don't hate being asked sensitive questions. So talking around difficult questions in research interviews is a waste of time and money.

Be bold with your questions while still being respectful. Never directly ask an individual a difficult question in a group context; instead, ask the whole group and wait patiently for an answer. People hate embarrassing silence, so someone will respond and 99% of the time others will probably follow, adding their own experience and perspective. Wait until at least halfway through the session to ask a difficult question, as you need to have established an atmosphere of cordial openness and sympathy in the group.

The last piece of advice I have is never presume that you have all the questions. For example, after a team has presented a worksheet, ask the group whether there are any more questions about the work. Their perspective is different to yours and often if someone has a question it will be something you hadn't thought of.

1% being a catalyst

A moderator must be both neutral and a black hole of ignorance; however, like a tiny pinch of spice that can transform a recipe, a little nudge can open great avenues of unexplored territory. Nudging, in small quantities and with discretion, requires balance and restraint. To borrow a phrase from French photographer Robert Doisneau, 'To suggest is to create; to describe is to destroy.' He was referring

---

[32] E. Hart, E. VanEpps and M. E. Schweitzer, 'I didn't want to offend you: The cost of avoiding sensitive questions' (2019), SSRN, https://papers.ssrn.com/sol3/papers.cfm?abstract_id=3437468 [accessed 2 June 2020].

to creating images, not moderating Collaborative Creativity sessions, but I think those words capture the fine line between inspiring and influencing.

A moderator shouldn't make suggestions but is expected to ask questions and, as I have stated previously, creativity is 50% problem solving and 50% asking the right questions. By asking the right question, you can help the group to see things from a novel perspective, highlighting incongruences or overlooked aspects.

Always remember that the people in the room are the heroes – they are the experts. A moderator is just an agitator of people and talents. A good moderator must influence the thinking of the group and their work as little as possible, but when needed they should influence the focus of the thinking and remind the group of their objective and its scope.

People are often limited by self-imposed boundaries. The design of the exercises should help push these boundaries, but a moderator can ask, for example, why a team's ideas are all within a certain domain and why they aren't exploring further afield.

Over the course of the session, a good way to do this is by following the example of others. If one team has explored an interesting area that others have ignored, encourage everyone to reutilize, repurpose, incorporate and expand the ideas from other teams. Ask teams what would happen if they took their idea in a particular direction, like another team has. The dynamics of this can be really interesting and productive.

I've often seen a team take another team's idea and make something more interesting from it while the team that created the original idea didn't make any progress with it at all. Sometimes we can't see all the potential of our own ideas.

100% listening

All the above is meaningless if the moderator isn't attentive and a good listener (to both verbal and non-verbal language). It is the moderator's responsibility to document and produce a record of what happens in the session, but it shouldn't be done alone. Taking extensive notes is something that can and should be done in parallel with colleagues. We all have our own biases, and these influence both perception and memory. A moderator must write down what they see and hear as soon as possible and it is important to have one or more moderator simultaneously take their own notes. Only by confronting two, or better still three, sets of notes after the session can you be reasonably certain that you have faithfully captured the events as they occurred.

Deposition

I have borrowed a legal term (for a formal, written statement to be used as evidence) to underline the seriousness of this last responsibility of the moderator.

Every Collaborative Creativity session must have its own written report, which includes images of all the worksheets produced during the session. At the end of a session, each moderator must have their own set of notes and they must photograph all the worksheets before collecting them. Photographing is important because, especially with collage exercises, when you get to the office and unpack the worksheets you might find pieces that have come unattached from their worksheets and, without photographic evidence of the original state of the object, you can never be sure of how to recompose it.

The basis of a written report is the moderator's notes. These must be written up within 24 hours of the end of the session. Even if the session is part of a series and the results will eventually be aggregated, it is important for each moderator present at a session to respect this rule. As I have already stated, our perception is imperfect and our memories are even more so. They deteriorate quickly over time. So, as soon as possible, all those who took notes must compare them and together create a chronological account of the events and output. Together with images of the worksheets, these are compiled to create the main part of the report.

The next task, in collaboration with the coach, is to analyse the output in relation to each of the key questions posed by the session and produce a description of the relevant results. The final task is to help the coach write a one-page executive summary of the session output. If the project contains just one session, then conclusions and recommendations are included in the session report, whereas for projects with various sessions, the conclusions and recommendations are included in the project report.

Change and opportunity

I wrote the first draft of this book in the last half of 2019 and I have found myself revising the manuscript in the first half of 2020, during the coronavirus pandemic. Suddenly, asking people to travel to a distant city and spend a day working in close contact with 20 or so other people has become absurd and even illegal.

The consequences of this emergency are so enormous that they are hard to comprehend. I offer just one statistic: as of 15 April 2020, governments in 191 countries had closed schools, affecting 1,600 million children worldwide according to UNESCO. The business professor Richard Rumelt calls historical events like the Long Depression of 1893–97 and the Great Depression of the 1930s, which mark momentous transition points of the economy and society, 'structural breaks'. It seems self-evident that the coronavirus crisis is a 'structural break' that will bring momentous change, and we will certainly face more volatile, uncertain, complex and ambiguous times ahead.

As I finish writing this book, I am busy experimenting with modes of remote creative collaboration, because the business of reinventing businesses is booming. At some point – hopefully not too far away – it will once again be safe to congregate. However, I am not alone in suspecting that the new normal will not be a wholesale return to the pre-pandemic normal. So, in this final chapter, let me play futurologist and attempt some predictions for how Collaborative Creativity will continue to be valuable for the pharmaceutical business.

Quality office time

The first consideration is how offices will change. The millions of people working from home during the pandemic have proven that, thanks to the technology we already possess, for many jobs having an office that accommodates every employee on every working day is a luxury. The pandemic has created an economic crisis and depression that will force all businesses to examine and drastically trim fixed costs – reducing office space will seem financially sound and be morally justified by a continued need for social distancing, at least until a cure or vaccine for the virus is discovered. Last year, large British companies paid on average approximately £4,000 per employee in annual rental costs and just 40–50% of desks were actually used during working hours.[33]

The technology we use for working-from-wherever will improve and most employees will adapt to a semi-virtualized working environment – semi-virtualized because there will still be a need for teams of colleagues to occasionally meet and examine important issues together, and to align their activities and approach.

At this point, what until recently was a standard type of meeting will no longer be fit for purpose. With people travelling specifically to meet (as opposed to travelling to go to work and the working day being full of meetings), and with much longer periods of time passing between one meeting and another, businesses and employees will need the time spent together to be more effective and productive.

Mass distraction

The same technology that has enabled working-from-wherever has also brought a debilitating information and communication overload. It is possible that permanent remote collaboration will exacerbate this problem, with even more time spent by each individual keeping up with and contributing to the tsunami of communications. It is

---

[33] Schumpeter [blog], 'Covid-19 is foisting changes on business that could be beneficial', *The Economist*, 5 March 2020, www.economist.com/ business/2020/03/05/covid-19-is-foisting-changes-on-business-that-could-be-beneficial [accessed 2 June 2020].

inevitable that the quality of the constant communication will suffer as the burden it represents increases.

Written word-based communications have the advantage of being asynchronous, and of leaving a permanent record, but they are a cold media and, especially when little time can be dedicated to reading or writing a message, they can easily lead to misunderstandings. Blaise Pascal wrote, 'I have made this [letter] longer than usual because I have not had time to make it shorter.'[34]

Phone calls and video calls are warmer forms of communication, but they have the disadvantage of being synchronous, ephemeral and, compared with a live meeting, they too are relatively cold and often frustrating.

I think many people will have noticed that cold, remote communication tools work better with people who have a pre-existing relationship and are more problematic when used with strangers. If the new normal relies on cold communication tools for daily exchanges, the quality of any periodic live meetings will need to increase greatly. Imagine initiating a new team member or beginning a complex project. These kinds of moments of collaboration will still need to be done live to be engaging and humanly rewarding, and they will need to offer, in a relatively short amount of time, better bonding and alignment of teams.

The soul in the machine

Distancing, work-from-wherever and virtualization will weaken or even destroy qualitative feedback loops. For example, if the field force is not in the field talking to doctors, who feels the pulse of the market? We are already awash with data and, as more communication shifts to digital platforms, there will be exponentially more data. This data will concern not only the market and all that is outside the company, but increasingly it will include data on employees. Where you are won't matter; rather, what you do will remain important and, with much of the day spent using digital platforms in some way, performance statistics will be tracked and analysed.

Businesses already use multiple sources of data to assess performance and identify opportunities within and outside the corporation. They

---

[34] Blaise Pascal, Letter XVI from *Lettres provinciales* (1657).

already use machine learning to find patterns and 'make sense' of gigantic pools of information. This will certainly continue and become increasingly sophisticated.

I believe there is a risk that with more data there will be more disconnect from the reality the data represents. The more isolated and removed we become from the context of the data, the less we understand what it means or could mean. Without high-quality intelligence that uncovers the irrational foibles of humanity, data alone will find humans inscrutable for decades to come.

Signal-to-noise ratio

Once you have found human meaning that has a significant impact on your business, how do you react to it? How do you make sure your team appreciates the consequence of this discovery? How do you go about adapting your business? How do you make sure the important things stand out from the urgent stuff?

To understand deep, rich concepts and their ramifications, we all need to concentrate and we need time. Quickly skimming a document or listening distractedly to Cortana or Siri read out loud is not a solution. Finding the time and mental space to absorb important ideas and elaborate them with colleagues and other stakeholders will become a struggle. Aligning the mindset of a group and managing or leading change will become more difficult with a physically separated workforce. Identifying ways of navigating the agile office – a condensed, fluid environment – will require the inclusion of skills and rituals that allow a group to retreat, regroup and refocus effectively before they react. Effective and honest collaboration will be needed to ensure that the resulting actions are not only beneficial for the enterprise but also have positive and desirable effects upon the healthcare system, caregivers and, above all, patients.

Plastic brains

There are many digital natives in the workforce today, and over time they will become the totality. These people have an advantage in using digital tools of all kinds compared with those who had to adapt and learn new skills and attitudes.

Imagine the same dynamic with distancing. A generation from now, there may be distancing natives in the workforce, but today there are none. Everyone is adapting and learning new skills. The impact of this is psychological as much as it is practical.

Our brains are able to change and adapt as a result of experience – this is known as *neuroplasticity*. But neurological adaptation takes time and requires repetition, which is why learning something like how to play a musical instrument is so slow. It is why the transition to the next normal in office collaboration will be one of the most ambitious change-management projects ever attempted. I think it will require alignment and co-authoring for it to become a real culture of brains that have successfully adapted together.

Trains and helicopters

At work, we are all like trains, trying to run to schedules, tethered to tracks that dictate our range of activity and rushing forward at ever greater speed. We can presume this is productive and relatively efficient because that is how we all work – people and businesses have all evolved to perform in a similar way.

But every now and then it is important for a train to become a helicopter for a day – hovering, observing, climbing to benefit from a completely different perspective. The tracks that were our domain become lines snaking over a terrain and a big picture is revealed that changes our perception of what it means to be a train when we return to the tracks the following day and the day after that. If you hire people to think and not just do, on occasion you have to let their minds fly.

Julia Rozovsky is an analyst with Google People Operations (Google's term for Human Resources). She set out to find out what makes a team great. After two years of work and over 200 interviews with Google employees, tracking more than 250 attributes of 180 different teams, she introduced the results of her work with this phrase, 'Who is on a team matters less than how the team members interact, structure their work, and view their contributions.'[35]

---

[35] J. Rozovsky, 'The five keys to a successful Google team', re:Work, 17 November, https://rework.withgoogle.com/blog/five-keys-to-a-successful-google-team [accessed 2 June 2020].

By now, you know that Collaborative Creativity is all about how team members interact, structure their work and view their contributions. The way we work is important. It matters for corporate performance and it matters for the wellbeing and happiness of the individuals who work for corporations.

The way we work today influences the things we create and the things we create today shape our future. I hope that if you do use the information in this book, you can use it to shape a better present and build a better future.

Further resources

The templates mentioned in this book and various exercise formats are available from my website: https://peter-comber.net/collaborativecreativity. If you would like to get in touch with me, please use the contact form on the website.

The ideas in this book were formed by practical experience but also shaped and confirmed by the ideas of others through the magic medium of books. The following is a list of enlightening titles that are in some way connected to the ideas presented in this book.

Further reading on how we think and act

Anna Abraham, *The Neuroscience of Creativity* (2018)

Dan Ariely, *The (Honest) Truth About Dishonesty: How We Lie to Everyone – Especially Ourselves* (2012)

Dan Ariely, *Predictably Irrational: The Hidden Forces that Shape Our Decisions* (2008)

Antonio R. Damasio, *Descartes' Error: Emotion, Reason, and the Human Brain* (2006)

David Eagleman, *Incognito: The Secret Lives of the Brain* (2016)

Malcolm Gladwell, *Talking to Strangers: What We Should Know About the People We Don't Know* (2020)

Daniel Kahneman, *Thinking, Fast and Slow* (2012)

Shane Parrish, *The Great Mental Models, Volume 2: Physics, Chemistry and Biology* (2020)

Robert Trivers, *The Folly of Fools: The Logic of Deceit and Self-Deception in Human Life* (2014)

Matthew Willcox, *The Business of Choice: How Human Instinct Influences Everybody's Decisions*, 2nd edition (2020)

Further reading on creativity

Claire Bridges, *In Your Creative Element: The Formula for Creative Success in Business* (2016)

Tim Brown, *Change by Design: How Design Thinking Transforms Organizations and Inspires Innovation* (2019)

Mihaly Csikszentmihalyi, *Creativity: Flow and the Psychology of Discovery and Invention* (2013)

Edward de Bono, *Six Thinking Hats* (2000)

Stefanie Jansen and Maarten Pieters, *The 7 Principles of Complete Co-Creation* (2017)

Matthew Syed, *Rebel Ideas: The Power of Diverse Thinking* (2019)